THE CARE AND
FEEDING
OF IDEAS

THE CARE AND FEEDING OF IDEAS

A Guide to Encouraging Creativity

James L. Adams

author of CONCEPTUAL BLOCKBUSTING

ADDISON-WESLEY PUBLISHING COMPANY, INC.

Reading, Massachusetts · Menlo Park, California
Don Mills, Ontario · Wokingham, England
Amsterdam · Bonn · Sydney · Singapore · Tokyo
Madrid · Bogotá · Santiago · San Juan

Permission to reprint or adapt illustrations was obtained from the following sources:

Page ii Drawing by André Francois; © 1958 by André Francois. Courtesy of John Locke Studios, Inc., New York.

Page 2 Drawing by J. J. Sempé; © 1980 by The New Yorker Magazine, Inc.

Page 12 Drawing by Elwood H. Smith; © 1974 by Elwood H. Smith. Courtesy of the artist and *TriQuarterly*, a publication of Northwestern University.

Page 14 Drawing by Deborah Warren. Other drawings by Ms. Warren appear on pages 66, 67, 74, 92, 166, 181, and 201.

Page 26 Painting by Harou Miyauchi; © The Pushpin Group, Inc., New York.

Page 30 Illustration by David A. Macaulay from *The Amazing Brain* by Robert Ornstein, Richard F. Thompson, and David A. Macaulay; illustration © 1984 by David A. Macaulay. Reprinted by permission of Houghton Mifflin Company.

Continued on facing page

Many of the designations used by manufacturers and sellers to distinguish their products are claimed as trademarks. Where those designations appear in this book and Addison-Wesley was aware of a trademark claim, the designations have been printed in initial capital letters (e.g., Chicken McNuggets).

Library of Congress Cataloging-in-Publication Data

Adams, James L.
   The care and feeding of ideas.

   Includes index.
   1. Creative thinking. 2. Change (Psychology)
3. Problem solving. I. Title.
BF408.A3   1986   153.3′5   86-10895
ISBN 0-201-10160-2
ISBN 0-201-10087-8 (pbk.)

Cover design by R.O. Blechman
Text design by Anna Post, Chicago, IL
Set in 10 point Palatino by DEKR Corporation, Woburn, MA

BCDEFGHIJ-DO-8987
Second Printing, January 1987

Page 36   Drawing by Barbara Frake, adapted from "Brain Function and Blood Flow" by Neils A. Lassen, David H. Ingvar, and Erik Shinoj, *Scientific American*, October 1978. Adapted by permission of W.H. Freeman and Company.

Page 42   Drawing adapted from *Sensation and Perception* by Richard H. Schiffman; © 1976 by John Wiley & Sons, Inc. Adapted by permission of John Wiley & Sons, Inc.

Page 44   M.C. Escher, *Other World*, 1947, wood engraving; © by M.C. Escher Heirs. Courtesy of Cordon Art, Baarn, Holland.

Page 45 (top)   Drawing adapted from *The Intelligent Eye* by R.L. Gregory; © 1970 by R.L. Gregory. Adapted by permission of McGraw-Hill Book Company.

Page 45 (bottom)   Drawing from *Psychology* by Henry Gleitman; © 1981 by W.W. Norton & Company. Reprinted by permission of W.W. Norton & Company.

Page 46   Salvador Dali, *The Slave Market with Disappearing Bust of Voltaire*, 1940, oil on canvas. Courtesy of the Salvador Dali Museum, Saint Petersburg, Florida.

Page 47   Photograph of a spotted dog by Ronald C. James from *The Intelligent Eye* by R.L. Gregory; © 1970 by R.L. Gregory.

Page 54   René Magritte, *L'homme au journal*, 1927, oil on canvas; © 1987 by Charly Herscovici, Brussels. Courtesy of the Tate Gallery.

Page 68   Painting by Joo Chung; © 1986 by Joo Chung.

Page 71   Diagram from *Human Memory*, second edition, by Roberta Klatzky; © 1980 by W.H. Freeman and Company. Reprinted by permission of W.H. Freeman and Company.

Page 74   Graph adapted from "The Variation of Memory with Time for Information Appearing During a Lecture" by E.J. Thomas, *Studies in Adult Education*, Volume 4, Number 1, April 1972.

Page 84   Drawings from *What People Wore* by Douglas Gorsline; © 1952, 1980 by Douglas Gorsline. Reprinted by permission of Viking Penguin, Inc.

Page 89   Photograph of John Adams, the author's brother. Courtesy of John Adams.

Page 104   Drawing by George Booth; © 1978 The New Yorker Magazine, Inc.

Pages 110 & 199   Photographs courtesy of James L. Adams.

Page 111   Drawing by Jim M'Ginness from *Conceptual Blockbusting*, third edition, by James L. Adams; © 1974, 1976, 1979, 1986 by James L. Adams. Reprinted by permission of Addison-Wesley Publishing Company, Inc.

Page 113   Drawing by Christopher Carduff, after Jim M'Ginness.

Page 201 Chart adapted from *The New Rational Manager* by Charles H. Kepner and Benjamin B. Tregoe; © 1981 by Kepner-Tregoe, Inc. Reprinted by permission of Kepner-Tregoe, Inc., Princeton, New Jersey, specialists in strategic and operational problem solving and decision making.

Page 210 Drawing by J.C. Suares from *The Devil's Dictionary* by Ambrose Bierce; illustration © 1979 by J.C. Suares. Reprinted by permission of Harper & Row, Publishers, Inc.

Permission to quote material from various books was obtained from the following sources:

Pages 81 & 82 Quotes from *Memory* by I.M.L. Hunter; © 1957, 1964 by Ian M.L. Hunter. Reprinted by permission of Penguin Books Ltd.

Pages 93 & 94 Quotes from "The Two Cultures and the Scientific Revolution" by C.P. Snow; © 1959 by C.P. Snow. Reprinted by permission of Cambridge University Press.

Page 99 "Sketch of Freud's Stages of Psychosexual Development in the Male" adapted from *Psychology* by Henry Gleitman; © 1981 by W.W. Norton & Company, Inc. Adapted by permission of W.W. Norton & Company, Inc.

Pages 107 & 108 Quotes from *How to Solve It* by George Polya; © 1945, 1973 by Princeton University Press. Reprinted by permission of Princeton University Press.

Pages 108 & 109 Quotes from *Applied Imagination*, third edition, by Alex Osborn; © 1963 by Charles Scribner's Sons. Reprinted by permission of Charles Scribner's Sons.

Page 112 Quote from *The Universal Traveler* by Don Koberg and Jim Bagnall; © 1974 by William Kaufman, Inc. Reprinted by permission of William Kaufman, Inc.

Page 154 "Erikson's Eight Stages of Man" adapted from *Childhood and Society* by Erik H. Erikson; © 1963 by Erik H. Erikson. Adapted by permission of W.W. Norton & Company, Inc.

Page 187 "A Synectics Excursion" by Jonathan Prince; © 1980, 1985 by Synectics, Inc. Reprinted by permission of George M. Prince.

Page 204 Quote from *Strategies for Change* by James Brian Quinn; © 1980 by Richard D. Irwin, Inc. Reprinted by permission of Richard D. Irwin, Inc.

**To Jean Adams
and the memory of Lowell Adams
who cared for and fed
me**

Contents

Preface

This book has to do with control of the new and unusual; it discusses rational action in unprecedented situations. It is aimed towards those who attempt to better manage creativity and change. This should include all of us, whether we do so as a profession, simply to better enjoy life, or both. Creativity and change take us into the unknown — where our experience and expertise may not be as valid as when we are engaged in more traditional pastimes. It deals with situations where we must, in a sense, fly by instruments since our intuition is not always trustworthy; where misleading intellectual and emotional signals may degrade decision making, communication, and education.

Can we manage in situations involving creativity and change? Obviously, we can. We cannot manage so well that we obtain the low risk levels and high efficiency associated with traditional activities. However, we can certainly improve upon the type of performance resulting from random moves or old patterns applied in a new game. If we are paddling down a new river and come upon rapids, we should steer through them as best as possible. We should neither steer the same course as we used in past rapids nor should we pull in our paddle and just let the boat go. Fortunately, there is a good bit of knowledge that lets us steer through new rapids quite well. This knowledge is the subject matter of this book.

This is not an academic book based entirely on research and fact, although it references research and fact and I will be glad to take on any argument. Creativity and change are difficult to study and almost by definition not completely understood. We are best at understanding things that repeat over time. Our knowledge and techniques are generally based on the steady state or on predictable rates of change. Creativity implies something without precedent. Real change is not predictable. We are therefore in a land of conjecture. However, I have been living professionally in this land as engineer, manager, consultant, and educator for thirty years now, have had my share of successes and failures, and have become convinced that there is a large amount of specific knowledge and technique of great value in managing creativity and change. I have also lived in a very nonboring half-century and am convinced that these lessons can be applied to professional and nonprofessional situations alike.

This is a middle-of-the-road book as far as the costs and benefits of managing creativity and change are concerned. It places little stock in "free lunches." There are real costs associated with increasing creativity. I am an optimist concerning the potential of better managing creativity and change but I have yet to be involved in a miracle.

It is also a middle-of-the-road book in tone. These days there is much ado about creativity and change. A look at the best-seller lists for the past few years substantiates this (see the bibliographic material in Chapter 13). So do conversations with human resource development managers in organizations or a look at the pages of business magazines, which presently abound with pleas for innovation, entrepreneurship, and economic victory over various other nations. There are good reasons for this present preoccupation, of course, since many of the foundations on which we have based our lives (the US position in world trade and policy, the traditional family, the two eggs and bacon breakfast) have tottered. Expectations of many portions of society have risen and at the same time we have become aware of the finite nature of resources and the delicate nature of our ecology. We have also bought ourselves a mixture of hopes, fears, and uncertainties with the startling advances of science and technology.

However, we have been enraptured with creativity and change in the past. When I was first introduced to the topic by a charismatic gentleman named John Arnold in the 1950s, there was much going on. There were certain similarities to this period in that business was adjusting (between wartime and peacetime economies) and there was concern about nuclear armageddon (the Berlin crisis and bomb shelters). There were also different concerns then, such as that about conventionality, discussed repeatedly in print by writers such as Vance Packard, Paul Goodman, and William Whyte. Social concern with creativity and change was in full flower. There were national workshops and established education groups, consultants and industry training courses. There was a great amount of writing. In 1964, Taher A. Razik, then with the Creative Education Foundation at the State University of New York in Buffalo, published a bibliography of creative studies that contained over 4,000 items. Half of them had been written since 1950. Those of you who were interested in such things during the time probably remember some of the theories of Abraham Maslow, Carl Rogers, Alex Osborn, Sidney Parnes, John Arnold, Frank Barron, William J.J. Gordon, Arthur Koestler, and Lawrence Kubie.

There was a decrease in attention to creativity and change between the middle 1960s and the late 1970s. The social turmoil in the late 1960s turned much of the United States to a yearning for tradition and peace. The Vietnam war gave us philosophical and ethical problems to brood about. The turmoil over civil rights, OPEC, inflation, and our new difficulty in international competition further dampened our national spirit. However, when it became evident that things would not revert to a simpler time and that we really had no alternate, we again became challenged by change and the need for increased cleverness.

As our interest in creativity and change has waxed and waned, we have consistently learned more about creativity and change and their management. This book is an overview of some of the principles involved. It is tuned neither toward periods of obsession with creativity and change nor toward periods of neglect. If you are reading it now because creativity and change are "in" topics, fine. However, it is not efficient to attempt constantly to turn the fires of creativity up and down. Therefore, take this book off of the shelf and read it again when no one is talking about creativity and change. It will be equally, if not more, pertinent. The wildly varying attention paid to creativity and change over time is in itself a symptom of poor management.

Some acknowledgments are very much in order at this time. I would first like to thank all of the students, industry people, teachers, and others with whom I have been able to interact over the years. Without such interaction it would have been impossible to put this material together. I would like to thank Professor Harold Leavitt of the Stanford Graduate School of Business, Professor Albert Hastorf and Professor Jeffry Wine of the Stanford Psychology Department, and Barry Katz of the Stanford Program in Values, Technology, Science, and Society, for reading portions of the manuscript in order to tell me whether the thin ice upon which I was venturing was developing fatal cracks. Next, I would like to thank Robert Lavelle, the editor of this book and a wonderful collaborator. His ability to become interested in the material was phenomenal, as was his ability to find the way through tangles. His role was so active that I should also probably thank IBM for producing the computer that allowed me to implement his suggested manuscript changes without going mad. I would also like to thank Christopher Carduff, who ably picked up the project when Bob moved on to other pastures. Finally, I would like to thank my wife Marian and our children, Bob, Dan, Sam, and Elizabeth. Marian not only "read my damn book twenty times," but makes my whole life wonderful. Our children, like most, are living breathing examples of the challenge of being creative in a conservative world. Their interest and success in becoming unique individuals in a society that sometimes acts like it wants everyone to be the same is a testimony that good guys win and creativity has an unlimited future. Watching them has helped keep me fascinated with this topic. Now, on to the book.

THINKING

1

Introduction to Creativity
and Change

This book is about new directions . . . about dealing rationally and creatively with unprecedented situations. In one way or another, each day presents us with unprecedented situations. *We are all creative and we all change* — this is the stuff of life. If this were not the case, we simply could not endure.

Creativity and change are two sides of the same coin. They are often linked, in that creativity is needed to respond successfully to change and creativity, in turn, results in change. Creativity and change both imply new directions. They are both associated with uncertainty and risk. They result in similar emotional and cultural responses. There is anxiety, fear, and disapproval associated with newness. However, there is also joy, excitement, and approval. Creativity and change imply deviance, and we are schizophrenic about deviance. We both applaud it and worry about it. We both seek it and seek to avoid it.

This book is about deviating. In particular, it has to do with managing ourselves and others better in new situations. Why should we care about this topic? This book could easily be devoted to answering this question, but I give you credit for knowing the answer. Part of it has to do with the fact that new directions win for us. It is creativity that allows us to better our lot. It allows the hunter-gatherer to acquire a larger pile of spoils with decreased effort and risk. It allows the subsistence farmer to dedicate less of life to sweating in the sun. It allows Tom Sawyer to get his aunt's fence whitewashed without effort (and with a profit), and Brer Rabbit, the three little pigs, and Theseus to escape death.

New directions also have to do with self-satisfaction. Creativity has something to do with being smart. We want to express our unique capabilities and feelings. Creativity is important. It feels good. If we were placed on an idyllic desert island completely stocked with all luxuries, we would eventually create something new for ourselves. A certain amount of change also feels good. If the water is too flat, we make waves. Most of you are probably achievement-oriented people, in that you derive satisfaction from reaching goals. However, that does not necessarily mean that you derive equal satisfaction from the goal itself. You may like hunts better than foxes. If that is the case, you are probably familiar with the process of setting a goal, reaching it, becoming delighted, then depressed, and setting another goal. This is a common pattern with the professional who has "made it." A new "it" seems to be necessary to keep the ride going. One can read all about motivations for new directions in psychology books, but it is not necessary to go that far. Just look at your own life. Would you like to be a little more creative? Most people will answer that question in the positive. Why? Have you ever thought you needed a change in your life? Why? Increased creativity and change do not lead directly to increased relaxation and graciousness. There must be something deeper involved.

THE WORLD IS ALWAYS CHANGING

This book focuses on *changes* in our level of creativity and ability to respond to change. Not only do we seek more creativity and change for winning and for stimulation, but our environment also changes over time and, if we do not accommodate, the strain becomes intolerable. An example of an environmental factor that changes is the economy. The inflationary cycle experienced by those living in the United States in the 1970s affected everyone deeply. Yet, as individuals, groups, and large organizations, we could not effectively control it. Other examples of environmental factors are social changes that affect our living habits. In a fascinating book entitled *How We Live*, Victor Fuchs, an economist, studied society in the United States during the past few decades. His data is startling, especially if you think that 1950 was not all that long ago. During the time period

1950 to 1980, the percentage of married women with children under six years of age who were wage earners increased from 12 to 45 percent. The proportion of adults living alone almost tripled, and the proportion of men sixty-five years of age and older in the labor force fell by more than half. In 1950, one child in ten did not live with two parents. In 1980, the proportion was closer to one child in four. Between 1950 and 1975 the divorce rate doubled. I will not continue to give examples here, but reading Fuchs' book illuminates large numbers of sweeping changes, which, whether we approve or not, are upon us. The world is changing in major ways, and we must either change with it or become increasingly frustrated.

Changes in our environment can overwhelm us if we do not move rapidly enough. Each year statistics accompany the publication of the list of Fortune 500 companies that show changes in the list. The number of companies that are taken off the list is large. Few of those companies leave the list voluntarily. They are surpassed by companies who move more skillfully in a changing environment.

There are certainly bounds to our ability to be creative and to change. If the rate is too rapid, we are in trouble. Individuals living in the midst of too much newness and too little tradition suffer. Many of us felt some of this during the late 1960s when people seemed to be attempting to destroy too many of the old standard beliefs, systems, and social customs. Too much creativity on the individual level can lead to a nervous breakdown. Too much creativity in a company can lead to bankruptcy. Any company employing engineers can make that test easily by giving them all of the support they ask for to develop new products and services. Too little creativity similarly leads to failure — noncompetitiveness in business and boredom in the individual.

There are strong motivations toward change and creativity. However, there are also strong inhibitions against them. These motivations and inhibitions will be considered in detail because they lead us to mechanisms to better manage creativity and change. Whether we are an individual, a group, or a large organization, we are in balance between motivations and inhibitions. This balance may not be consistent with our goals and may not be sensitive to changes in the environment. It may reflect past influences rather than future desires. We can perhaps win by changing this status quo — by tipping the balance. This tipping implies management.

It is important to realize that we might desire to tip the balance in either direction. We might want to decrease creativity and change in our lives in order to obtain stability and control. This book generally speaks to increasing creativity and change, since people who pick up books such as this usually have that in mind. However, the principles and techniques in the book work frighteningly well in reverse. Just as reward can encourage creativity, so too can punishment discourage it. Depriving creative people of resources slows them down just as effectively as the provision of resources aids them. Chopping the R&D budget will result in fewer products and, therefore, lower product development costs. Rewarding children for memorizing their geography instead of practicing with their rock band may result in higher grades. However, be warned that intentional attempts to decrease creativity, although possibly resulting in desired goals in the short term, usually result in long-term problems.

THE NATURE OF CREATIVITY

We will not spend a lot of time attempting to define creativity because it is a difficult task and we all have a reasonably good feeling for the meaning of the word. However, I have a particularly pragmatic view of creativity that will be reflected in this book, and a few general comments on the subject are in order here. First of all, we certainly expect something new to result from creativity. It is possible to bicker about the meaning of the word *new*. However, it is sufficient to define the word with respect to the people involved. It is true that if I reinvent the wheel, I will not obtain the usual advantages accruing to the inventor of a brand new device. However, it is probable that I will experience all of the throes of creativity up to the point where I realize that someone was there first. Even in situations where invention is not an issue, creativity can flourish in complex situations. Should the Chevrolet division of General Motors begin to manufacture a line of lingerie, a great amount of corporate creativity would be involved, even though the products would not be without precedent.

For the purpose of this book, we also expect the world to be different as a result of creativity. We will not be too interested in unimplemented concepts, since they are fairly easy to come by and not as much fun as concepts that are carried to the stage where they affect our lives. This is a critical discrimination, since many creativity books are concerned with the encouragement of ideas per se. In 1974, I wrote a book about creative problem solving called *Conceptual Blockbusting: A Guide to Better Ideas*. Since then, I've been lecturing to businesses, schools, government agencies, and other organizations on how to increase creativity and better respond to change. But over the years I've become increasingly frustrated with the belief that more ideas alone mean better results. If you're serious about encouraging creativity in yourself or others and if you want to deal with change effectively, then implementing ideas is at least as important as generating ideas. You need to understand the entire process — from concept to reality. Ideas are certainly important, both to define goals and to achieve them effectively. However, there are few "free lunch" ideas (how to get there without time, effort, and risk). Creativity requires that ideas be implemented, and it is in the pragmatic details of implementation that creativity often fails, relegating the ideas to occasional hindsight discussions at cocktail parties.

We will also be concerned with the creativity of people like us, rather than the Leonardos, Beethovens, and Einsteins. This is no great loss, since most of us have never met a Leonardo, a Beethoven, or an Einstein. Few of us possess the unusual blend of ability and motivation that causes individuals to so dramatically exceed the norm and, if we did, few of our institutions would hire us. We will be more interested in the performance of people nearer to social and psychological norms.

This will cause us to focus on conscious attempts to intervene directly in the creative process. A fascinating (but technical) book by Teresa Amabile entitled *The Social Psychology of Creativity* looks at creativity among people and concludes that we are more creative if left alone to do what we love. Her book centers around what she calls the intrinsic motivation hypothesis of creativity: the intrinsically motivated state is conducive to creativity, whereas the extrinsically motivated state is detrimental. In other words, we are more creative if engaged in a task that is inherently challenging and fun rather than in one in which we are motivated by needs for material gain, status, affiliation, defense, etc. It is easy to believe this hypothesis. In fact all of us would rather work on a task that is fun and challenging than a task that is merely work. We would expect the outstanding artist or the extraordinarily creative person to demand and achieve a life with a high amount of intrinsic reward.

However, for most of us, creativity is motivated both intrinsically *and* extrinsically. We can operate partially unconsciously and naturally (working on our hobbies, working in our favorite specialty) but must "push" at other times. If we want to increase the creativity in our lives, we should try to move toward activities where the reward is intrinsic. As William Shakespeare said, "No profit grows where is no pleasure taken, in short, study what thou dost affect." However, most of us are destined to remain heavily influenced by extrinsic motivations. This book will, therefore, focus on "pushing." For most of us, natural creativity is not enough. Most of us have an urge to accomplish things that do not happen naturally. The history of business entrepreneurship abounds with examples of people who once did extraordinarily well in a fairly natural way. For most of them, a high level of creativity was augmented by fortunate timing and a hospitable environment. For many of them, attempts to follow their initial success with others have not been as successful. Time and the environment changed, and their high natural creativity was not sufficient.

Similarly, we will not spend time on creative potential. Certainly we are different in our creative potential. However, it is not potential that limits us. It is the cost to us of trying to change the world. As we mentioned, most individuals could increase or decrease their creativity to the point where life was no longer satisfying, either because of anxiety or boredom. Most corporations could do the same, achieving death either by spending all of their capital on new ventures or by losing their ability to compete. In none of these cases would potential be an issue. We are more concerned with the process of increasing or decreasing creativity than with ultimate limits.

Finally, of course, we expect creativity to result in something that is "better" for us. Once again, we will use those involved in the creative effort as our reference. By doing this, we ignore ethical issues stemming from situations in which the creativity of a group or individual decreases the quality of the lives of others. We will assume that the development of the atomic bomb was a creative act because it accomplished something at the time seen as "better" for those involved.

GROUPS ARE MADE UP OF INDIVIDUALS

This book is concerned with creativity and change in individuals, groups, and large organizations. Individual creativity and change are essential to our discussion because they give us insight into creativity and change in general and because each of us acts as an individual. Creativity and change in groups and large organizations are important because we are not alone in our societies. We interact with others at home, at work, at school, in our social lives, and in pursuing our interests. Large organizations affect all of us, and many of us receive our paychecks from them. We will initially be concerned with creativity and change in the individual. As we proceed, however, more group factors will be introduced. Finally we will consider material essential to the management of creativity and change in large organizations.

INCREASING CREATIVITY REQUIRES WORK

Throughout this book you will occasionally be asked to do short exercises. PLEASE DO THEM!! Merely reading the exercises and hypothesizing about the outcome will do you little good. Books on memory improvement and physical exercise may be interesting to read, but you will become neither a better Trivial Pursuit player nor slimmer unless you do the exercises. This book is similar.

In fact, increasing creativity in general requires work. Undoubtedly you have stumbled across the old saying that creativity is 10 percent inspiration and 90 percent perspiration. The cynical claim is that inspiration is 90 percent perspiration and, therefore, the perspiration content in creativity must be 99 percent. In any case, the pragmatic viewpoint (which I agree with) is that increasing creativity and change requires conscious mental effort and resources. If you are a follower of the type of creativity techniques that are oriented toward producing alternate concepts (ideas), you probably have noticed that many of them call for the expenditure of conscious mental effort.

List-making is a popular conceptualization technique. It utilizes the construction of lists as a method of forcing alternative thinking. It is simple and extremely effective, especially if used in a competitive way (either against others or against ourself).

As an indication, try the following exercise:

EXERCISE

Spend three minutes making a list as long as you can of uses for ordinary yellow wooden pencils.

I could have as easily asked you to merely spend three minutes thinking of alternate uses for ordinary yellow wooden pencils without recording your ideas or to think of uses and jot them down as they occurred. It should be evident that the approach in the exercise is not only more effective at focusing your energy but also a more productive method of generating alternatives. It also requires and elicits a surprising amount of effort and produces more imaginative responses. Although eating pencils for roughage, constructing life preservers from them, moving pianos on them, and selling them to gophers for exercise devices may not be practical, imaginative responses tend to result from the type of effort induced by the exercise.

List-making can be as simple as "I am going to spend all day today thinking of as many ways as I can to get rid of household maintenance" or "Think of as many ways of mechanizing the function as you can" to as complex as "Carry five designs through the preliminary phase" or "We will have a three-day retreat at the beach to think about possible future product directions." List-making works by forcing the mind to dwell upon alternates to a greater extent than it normally would.

It is interesting to speculate on the success of such idea-stimulating techniques. They give us frameworks that allow us to consciously generate alternates that would not normally emerge from our unconscious. They exploit the fact that we are intellectually competitive, with ourselves as well as with others. When we make a list of ideas, we would like to make a long one and a good one. If we find that others make longer and better lists, we attempt to do better. Our western competitive ways, no doubt acquired in our schooling, work, and general socialization, help us here. This is interesting, since many creativity techniques, as we shall see later, are based on attempts to be less traditionally structured in our thinking; to be less "tough minded." Yet in list-making we have a situation where our structured routine habits can generate unusual concepts. List-making in its various guises improves our ability to generate concepts in a nonthreatening way. By causing us to exert effort, it allows us to generate more alternates than we otherwise would.

Why should perspiration (mental effort) be needed for creativity? How much is necessary and in what form? These are important questions. Creativity often falls short because the required effort and resources are not expended. The same can be said for the effectiveness of a book such as this. I have written it to be easily readable. However, if you want to get as much as possible from it, you will have to put some work into it.

The last chapter of this book contains bibliographic material for readers interested in pursuing the topic further. I recommend doing this very strongly. One of the primary difficulties in managing creativity and change is the unconscious nature of problem solving, which will be discussed in Chapter 2. We are not always aware of the thoughts occurring in our mind and in the minds of others. Reading causes us to become more aware of the nature of our thinking. Reading also provides us with the knowledge and understanding upon which we can build technique. Finally, reading about problem solving is fascinating, since there is no higher game than thinking about thinking. Philosophers have entertained themselves with this activity for years.

The first portion of this book is about thinking. In it we will take several looks at the habitual nature of human problem solving and inhibitions to increasing our creativity and responsiveness to change. This is not to imply that we are not creative. As I said before, we are. However, this approach has three advantages. First, looking at traditional steady state thinking gives us insight into creativity and change in the same way that examining conscious mental processes gives us insight into the unconscious. Second, the type of person who reads books like this resents being habitual in problem solving. Happily, the suggestion that we think in programmed and predictable ways causes most of us to attempt to disprove it by being creative. I am not above such cheap tricks. Finally, and most importantly, familiarity with this material allows us to understand the enemy (like Pogo said, "It is us."), the equipment we have at our disposal, and the need to steer ourselves consciously in new directions if we desire to increase our creativity. It also leads us to conclusions regarding the characteristics of effective steering.

The second part of this book is about doing. It focuses specifically on actions we may take to increase creativity and responsiveness to change, whether in the individual, group, or large organization. In a sense, this book proceeds from our heads to our world.

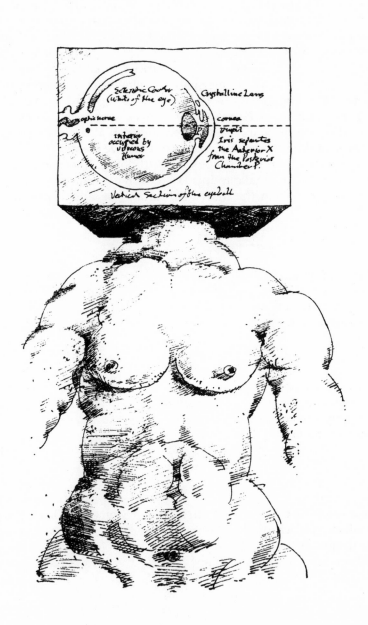

2

Some Thoughts about Thinking

One cannot talk about creative problem solving and response to change without coming up against unconscious thinking. Although it is mysterious because it cannot be directly observed, unconscious thinking is referred to again and again as "hunch," "incubation," "insight," and "intuition." Most accounts of creative acts refer to the appearance of concepts from someplace other than the consciousness (the "aha" reaction). For example, I was recently reading an article in an old science magazine about the development of the cosmological inflation theory. The first sentence was "Alan H. Guth has no idea why the equations began to come to him just when they did." Later on he is quoted as saying, "Actually, I think I was just very lucky. Without my knowing it the ideas were already in my head, and they seemed to come together in one fell swoop."

I was also recently rereading Tracy Kidder's excellent book *Soul of a New Machine* while preparing for a class discussion and came upon the episode he entitles "Wallach's Golden Moment." This is the point at which Wallach thinks of an elegant new architectural concept for the design of the computer, which is the project focus of the story. Wallach was drawing diagrams of possible ways to handle memory addresses and information security when he drew one that allowed him to use the same bits of information to define the address and the security level. This was a truly creative concept. What was Wallach's response? To quote Kidder, "As for Wallach, after he had drawn the diagram, he stared at it, wondering for a moment 'Where did that come from?' He kept eyeing it. 'That looks pretty cool.'" The following quote from the artist Peter Max is yet another testimony to the role of the unconscious: "I gaze at the canvas as my hand reaches for a brush and toward a color that pleases me. The painting begins. Color appears on the canvas. Squinting. Stretching. Splashing. Staring. I feel amazement. As an image is born it's as though I am actually standing behind myself watching someone else bring a canvas to life. I haven't planned it. Suddenly it's there."

Not only does the unconscious have something to do with the production of concepts, but it is also involved in the process by which we define problems and learn. Figure 2-1 is an interesting way of looking at the use of consciousness and unconsciousness in problem solving that I first saw being used in a talk by Chuck House, the Corporate Chief Engineer at Hewlett-Packard. He did not claim authorship of the figure. However, he was using it to claim (and I agree) that we follow a certain direction in learning to solve problems. He used the example of learning to tie our shoes. There is a certain time in life when we do not know how to tie our shoes but are unaware of it (unconscious and incompetent). We then reach a stage where we become aware that we do not know how to tie them (conscious and incompetent). We then learn to tie them (conscious and competent). Finally, tying our shoes becomes a habit (competent and unconscious). We know how to tie them, but do not need to think about it.

**FIGURE 2-1 From Unconscious Incompetence in Problem Solving
to Unconscious Competence**

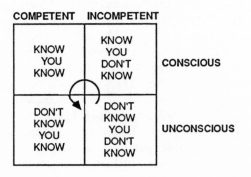

Learning requires that we first move from the lower right corner of Figure 2-1 to the upper right; we become conscious of what we do not know. Moving from the upper right to the upper left and then the lower left is familiar to us (classes, training, lessons) and fun if we are good at learning. However, we should notice that we end up back in highly unconscious territory. Living in the lower left is rewarding if we are blessed with good problem-solving habits, since we have control of our world. However, in order to increase creativity, we must be able to return to the upper right in order to begin the cycle again. We have to move from habit to an awareness of our ignorance. In order to do this, we may have to augment the unconscious with the conscious. Can we do this? Can we use our conscious mind to travel from our usual equilibrium corner (lower left) through the learning process again? You can tie your shoes unconsciously. Can you learn a new way to tie them unconsciously? Difficult! Can you learn a new way consciously? Aha — maybe there is hope. Obviously the relationship between unconscious and conscious is critical in managing creativity.

There is perhaps a more gut-level reason why we tend not to be as concerned with unconscious thinking as we should. It seems less "human" than conscious thinking. Why do we consider ourselves the most advanced of all organisms? Why do we place ourselves well above the bacteria, the mollusk, the termite, the beaver, and even the chimpanzee in the cosmic pecking order? Granted that we can stand erect and can boast opposed thumbs, but so can the chimpanzee. Granted that we are beautiful, but we secretly suspect that we might not appear as gorgeous to the wombat as we do to each other. We must conclude that, to the extent that we are unique and outstanding, we owe a debt to our consciousness.

We are blessed with a degree and type of consciousness that we have not been able to find among other forms of life. There are those who claim that the intelligence of other animals, of insect colonies, and even of plants has been underrated. There has been quite a bit of publicity in the past years about experiments with apes who have been taught to communicate in sign language and who show ability to combine these signs to show their feelings. There are similar efforts to understand the communication of dolphins. However, nowhere do we find serious hypotheses that other forms of life can in fact outthink humans or that they have a consciousness that allows the degree of abstraction, the prescience, the decision-making capability, or the imagination that we are aware of in our own lives. How do birds know how to build nests? Most people answer this question with "instinct" or a phrase indicating that nest-building is built into the genes of birds. We do not suspect that birds "think" while they build nests. We certainly do not think that they use blueprints, how-to-build-nest books, consultants, or any of the other trappings humans use in constructing a home. In fact, we would be terribly upset if we thought that they did. A discovery of this sort would permanently impair our taste for fried chicken.

It is no wonder that we come to think of ourselves in terms of our consciousness. Consciousness is synonymous with our awareness of experience. Conscious thinking is marvelous, if you think about it, if for no other reason than you can think about it. It is something we rely upon to carry out our lives and which brings us a tremendous sophistication in our ability to solve problems. We are justifiably proud of the free will and free choice that we exert through our consciousness, and this alone separates us from the other forms of life about us, which we consider to be less involved in conscious decision making and under the control of unconscious programming.

But how much of our problem solving is conscious? To what extent do we rely upon this unique conscious ability and to what extent are we, like the termites and beavers, creatures of habit and programming? To what extent is our problem solving unconscious?

In ·the nineteenth century, the concept of unconscious thinking was firmly established, at least in Europe. An influential book entitled *Philosophy of the Unconscious,* written by Eduard Von Hartmann in 1868 and revised through twelve editions, gives insight into some of the thinking of that time. It is based upon the philosophies of Hegel, Kant, and Schopenhauer, and refers to three levels of unconsciousness. The first, or "absolute," unconsciousness has to do with the nature of the universe and is the foundation of other layers. It is involved with the state of being. The second, or "physiological unconsciousness," is related to the evolutionary process and has to do with life. The third, or "psychological," unconsciousness is the basis of awareness and has to do with the life of man.

However, the founders of modern psychology did not like the concept of an unconscious at all. William James (1842–1910), who, in 1890, wrote the extraordinarily influential book *Principles of Psychology,* absolutely refuted the concept of a "thinking" unconscious. He had this to say about the concept of an unconscious: "It is the sovereign means for believing what one likes in psychology, and of turning what might become a science into a tumbling ground for whimsies." He then proceeded to list ten proofs for the existence of the unconscious and follow each one with objections. James stated, "There is only one phase in which an idea can be, and that is a fully conscious condition. If it is not in that condition, then it is not at all."

The early pioneers in psychology wanted to establish psychology as a science similar to physics. The concept of a "thinking" unconscious has traditionally been difficult for scientists to accept, if for no other reason than it cannot be observed. It is, in a sense, darkness that has not yet been illuminated by science. Even worse, it has historically been the base for all manner of mystic and supernatural explanations of human behavior and is, therefore, somewhat tarnished in the view of those who seek a more positivistic explanation of nature. It is even now not difficult to find people who are uncomfortable with the concept of a thinking unconscious.

In the middle of this attack on the concept of the unconscious came Sigmund Freud. He was primarily a clinician, although he was also one of history's greatest theoreticians. Although his theories were based upon his observation of patients, he certainly did not consider them at odds with science. He was very much aware of the viewpoint of James and his colleagues, but found it totally at odds with his own experiences and observations.

Freud argued that psychical processes exist that are not synonymous with conscious thinking. Psychoanalysis is based upon the theory that unconscious mental processes exist, although they cannot be directly observed by either the patient or the therapist. Yet unconscious mental processes can be inferred from observation and context. Whereas James and his friends argued that thinking took place in the conscious, Freud felt that it also took place in the unconscious; high level and complicated thinking occurred without the assistance of the consciousness. The academicians of the time, of course, attacked him for the contradictions contained in the notion of an "unconscious consciousness," but he counterattacked. In his book *Interpretation of Dreams*, published in 1900, he finished with a section on the unconscious and the conscious in which he stated that the unconscious is the basis of psychical life. He described the conscious as an imperfect window into the critical workings of the unconscious. He said "But what part is there left to be played in our scheme by consciousness, which was once so omnipotent and hid all else from view? Only that of a sense organ for the perception of psychical qualities."

Of course, this did not stop the debate about the unconscious. In the early 1900s, a group of people in Wurzburg, Germany, including Karl Buhler and R. S. Woodworth, began talking about imageless thought. They hypothesized that thinking existed that included images (visual, tactile, auditory, whatever) and thinking existed that did not. The latter type of thinking would obviously appear to be "unconscious" since the conscious is defined by its use of images that correspond to the senses. This is an appealing theory, since it relieves us of the need to consider the conscious and unconscious as separate. Thinking proceeds on its merry way and, for reasons of data limitation, importance, and function, some of it is blessed/encumbered with sensory imagery and some is not. It also gives us insights into certain aspects of thought that seem to be powerful and yet disembodied. Buhler wrote about experiments in which he asked his experimental subjects to respond to questions. They would often report that they understood a question and knew how well they could answer it before they could articulate a response. This type of thinking is familiar to students taking tests who are aware of how difficult each question is as they read it, how convincing their answers are as they write them, and how well they did at the end. It is the type of thinking that you do when I ask you Paul Newman's phone number. You know that you don't know.

Since the time of Freud and the Wurzburg group, other schools of thought have influenced psychology. Two of them that have been particularly influential and will be discussed in more detail later in this book are behavioral and cognitive psychology. The behaviorists were the most influential group in psychology for almost half of this century. However, their theory makes little use of concepts such as consciousness and unconsciousness. In fact, early behaviorists went so far as to deny the existence of "mind." In a paper entitled "Psychology as the Behaviorists View It" published in 1923, J. B. Watson (1878–1958) referred to two aspects of behaviorism: metaphysical and methodological. The methodological aspect insisted that humans are purely machines governed by learned response to stimuli. It denied not only the existence of "mind" but also "mental states," and claimed that conscious processes (called covert phenomena) were beyond the realm of scientific inquiry, if they existed at all. Watson, like James, insisted that psychology should proceed in the direction taken by the physical sciences and was strongly in favor of observation and against introspection and inference.

Behaviorists have mellowed since the time of Watson and now speak about the existence of "covert phenomenon." However, the mind and thinking are generally considered merely as mediators in the stimulus-response link. Behaviorists approach behavior directly in terms of "habit" learned through various combinations of repetition and reinforcement.

Cognitive psychologists, who are presently the emerging ruling class in academic psychology, are similar to the behavioral psychologists in that they do not rely on a Freudian unconscious as the basis of psychic activities. The cognitive psychologists view the mind as an information-processing device and tend to rely upon the concept of "attention" to deal with the conscious and the unconscious. One problem of the mind is the reduction of the overwhelming amount of data impinging upon the individual to a level that is usable in life. Attention refers to input that contributes directly to the conscious decision-making procedure (in this case, hopefully, the words you are reading). Other inputs are unconsciously monitored, but an attention controller may at any time bring these to the conscious (if, for example, someone were to drop a glass behind you). Cognitive psychologists have no difficulty with the concept of an unconscious, comfortable as they are with computers. Strangely enough, some of them seem to be more uncomfortable with the concept of conscious thinking.

What does all of this historical disagreement have to do with the management of creativity and change? It first of all points out the difficulty of working with the concept of unconscious thinking, which we must do. It also gives us an indication of why unconscious thinking is controversial and not too well understood. However, it also should substantiate what experience tells us is the case — both unconscious and conscious thinking exist.

James and his colleagues are somewhat alone in recent history. Other groups and schools of psychologists have viewed the concept of a "thinking" unconscious with attitudes ranging from disinterest (behaviorists) to zealous advocacy (psychoanalysts). The majority vote is clearly in favor of the ability of the brain to accomplish higher-order processing without conscious awareness. Similarly, with the exception of the hard-core behavioral and cognitive psychologists, we do not find much resistance to the concept of unconscious thinking. Even if it is difficult to explain in scientifically satisfying concepts, none of us would deny its existence. The existence of both conscious and unconscious thinking is certainly consistent with the existence of "habit" in problem solving; our mind relies upon a mixture of conscious and unconscious thought. The various psychological theories, old and new, also tell us extraordinarily valuable things about the characteristics of conscious and unconscious thinking. This information will appear throughout this book not only because it gives us insight into problem solving but also because it leads to techniques to exploit and modify intellectual habit.

Let us now see what we can conclude concerning the nature of conscious and unconscious mental processes by introspecting our own conscious thinking a bit and then implying a few things about the nature of unconscious activity from our knowledge of the capability of the mind. We can best do this through a short exercise.

E X E R C I S E

Simply attempt to catalog the activities that are occurring in your conscious mind — the mental palette used in conscious thinking. In particular, what types of languages and symbols do you use; how do the past, present, and future interact; and how and in what form do you recall information?

It is probable that you first noticed images corresponding to your senses: visual images; images of sound, smell, feeling, bodily sensation; whatever might have been appropriate to the thoughts you were thinking. In addition, you probably noticed one or more languages (you heard voices, either your own, other people's, or disembodied ones). You may also have experienced other abstract languages (mathematics, computer languages, double-entry bookkeeping, Morse code, etc.).

THE LIMITS OF CONSCIOUS AND UNCONSCIOUS THINKING

Conscious thinking deals with an abstraction of reality. It operates with the type of information that is typical of your life experience. It is not easy to deviate from the usual nature of such experience. Take speed, for instance. If you are thinking in "words," you are not greatly exceeding your reading speed, allowing for the fact that you do not need to move your eyes or turn pages. Recite something you know very well like the Gettysburg Address or the full names of your family members to yourself and see how rapidly you can do it. Conscious thinking proceeds in "real" time. To the extent that you can think about last year in five minutes, you are thinking in increments, similar to the way that movies are made.

Conscious thinking deals with information both from your senses and from your memory. These words you are reading are being sensed as you read. However, if you are aware of the sound of the words, that information is coming from your memory, since it is assuredly not coming from this page. If you look at your hand, you are processing information from your senses. If you close your eyes and imagine the face of your mother, you are using visual information stored in your memory. If you visit a restaurant that was a favorite of yours ten years ago and are disappointed, you are using a combination of information from your senses and from your memory.

Conscious thinking is also linear and single-channel in any sensory mode. It is occupied by one topic until it switches to another.

E X E R C I S E

Try thinking both about what you did yesterday and what you will do tomorrow.

Note that you had to do these sequentially, not simultaneously. You can switch back and forth rapidly, but you cannot do both tasks at precisely the same time.

Conscious thinking also prefers complete information. If you attempt to solve a complicated problem, for example, planning a nice evening for your family, your next vacation, or a company strategy to double profits, you will notice your conscious mind grasping for inputs from other sources and concluding that you need to "know" more to solve these problems.

Conscious thinking is limited by the nature of the information processing involved. In addition, as will be discussed later, it is influenced by purely emotional factors. The computer is oblivious to everything except its health and the details of the task at hand. This is not so with the human mind.

E X E R C I S E

Consciously imagine your favorite material possession. Now consciously imagine destroying it.

Did something happen? Sure. I originally focused this exercise on your pet animal. However, enough happened to my wife's mind when she read the draft of the book that I changed it.

Incidentally, we should not be jealous of the focus of the computer, although our lives are sometimes made complex by the constant mingling of the conscious and the unconscious. If a computer had been sitting under an apple tree when the apple hit it, it would not have printed out insights on the nature of gravity.

Let us discuss one more aspect of conscious thinking. Who (or what) controls it? Here is another exercise. It is an adaptation of one used to introduce people to meditation. It will not make you a meditator, but it will give you another interesting insight into your mind.

E X E R C I S E

Get a timer of some sort. Set it for three minutes, and during that time concentrate totally on your breathing. You will find your mind attempting to wander, so here is another task you can pursue at the same time. Count every third exhale. If you lose track, start over. Focus your mind totally on breathing and counting every third exhale.

What happened? A typical response is that your mind wandered anyway. You from time to time realized that you were thinking about yesterday or tomorrow; fantasizing; painfully aware of various sounds, smells, or other images; and occasionally needing to exert conscious effort to "force" your thinking back to your breathing. As I said, you have not been made into a meditator. (Any of you who do meditate were probably much better at this exercise. You can understand why if you look back at your experience in learning to meditate.) However, you have seen that the conscious mind is not always willing to do exactly what we might like it to. It is not merely a docile computer willing to respond to our whims.

If you are following me this far, you have been led into accepting a common misconception. Just who are "we"? Who attempts to control "our" minds? Do "I" control my conscious thinking, or is my conscious thinking "I"? The latter choice is closer to reality. Thinking of yourself in terms of some entity that "controls" conscious thinking is not consistent with the facts. Psychology books like to play around with the concept of the homunculus, a tiny person who we falsely credit with functions for which we do not have a good intuitive model. There is no homunculus controlling our conscious thinking. Conscious thinking evolved to better help us find food, avoid tigers, care for babies, find mates, and construct models of situations using sensory data. It is not about to sit idly by and concentrate totally on breathing. "I" and conscious thinking are all mixed up in life together and, try as we may, the mind will continue to wander when we wish it would not, to find alternate activities to avoid difficult ones (like writing books), and to respond rapidly to anything that implies danger.

To summarize, conscious problem solving:

- utilizes the experiential language of life
- is restricted in speed to a rate approximating that of life
- is linear and single-channel in any one sensory mode
- likes complete information
- is heavily influenced by behavioral factors
- does not always do what it (or "I," if you still prefer) might like it to do.

Now let us consider what it can do very well. First of all, without conscious thinking, the human experience could not be. On a slightly lower level, it allows the essential characteristics of human problem solving. It first of all permits us to *decide to do something and then attempt to do it*. This is our unique gift of free will and choice. During the problem-solving process, our conscious allows us to abstract life and build realistic constructs without actual experience. Daydreaming is a good example of this. Problem solving relies heavily upon this ability. Much of our problem solving consists of recalling past successes and "checking out" possible actions in our minds. It also allows us to communicate with each other. Because we share experiences and conscious thinking utilizes experience, we can communicate our conscious thoughts to each other. To add to the ability this gives us, we can use highly abstract languages (such as English or calculus) to convey information. Have no doubts that, as far as we are concerned, conscious thinking is not only the leading wonder of the world, but also the one with which we are most concerned. The only reason for the previous comments concerning conscious thinking is to suggest that, even though it is marvelous, it is neither omniscient nor impotent. There are some things it simply cannot do. We do need unconscious thinking.

If we attempt to explain the activities of our minds in terms of conscious process, we find immense voids. The exercises earlier in this chapter should have convinced you that data is sifted, combinations are made, decisions and conclusions are reached, and strategies are chosen without direct control of the conscious. These unconscious processes apparently work faster than our conscious ones, are better able to handle uncertainty, and are able to operate in nonlinear, multichannel modes (unlike the computer under the apple tree). They help us buy houses; change jobs; and aid in discovery, invention, innovation, and accommodation to change. However, since we are not generally aware of their existence, unconscious processes are "programming" in our minds, and we should realize that they make us habitual in our problem solving. The conscious is able to override them to some extent, provided that we know enough about our problem solving to consciously play the proper role at the proper time.

Before leaving the topic of unconsciousness, let me make a comment on dreaming. This is a subject that has not only been studied at length, but that is available to us in the form of experience. Many interesting aspects of dreaming have been discovered, and the book by W. C. Dement listed in the resource section is a fascinating and easy-to-read introduction. All of us dream, and spend roughly the same amount of our nights in doing so. However, we vary widely in our ability to recall dreams. Our dreams are complex and contain the same imagery that is used by our conscious mind (that is, the information of the senses). Dreams progress at the same speed as awake experience and to some extent include problem solving. There are classic tales of people solving their problems in dreams. Kekule conceived of the structure of the benzene ring after dreaming of snakes linked together head to tail. Coleridge claimed to have composed "Kubla Khan" in a dream. Experiments reported in Dement's book have concluded that problem solving does occur in dreams.

A friend of mine claims that when he is plagued by an unusually complicated problem, he makes an attempt to dream about it. Before drifting off to sleep, he'll say the problem out loud. He'll then review all the different aspects of the problem (the emotional as well as the intellectual ramifications) and again repeat the problem to himself before closing his eyes. He reports that one of three things invariably happens: he wakes up with a "eureka!" and reaches for a pencil and note pad; he wakes up, goes to work, and during the course of the day resolves the problem and makes surprising progress; or (and this is the real danger of this approach) he reflects so earnestly on the problem that he is unable to get to sleep.

Our dreams are not under the control of our conscious. Few people are aware of the fact that they are dreaming as their dreams occur and are able to input them willfully. Many of us have dreams that reflect previously conscious experience, but we are not consciously controlling our dreams as they unfurl. Therefore, dreams are one more piece of evidence that complex mental activities occur, akin to those used in problem solving, without conscious control.

From this discussion of the conscious and the unconscious, we see that we have a unique and marvelous set of capabilities that allows us to solve problems in our distinctly human fashion. However, this discussion also leads us to suspect that we are habitual in our problem solving, including our creativity and response to change, since unconscious thinking plays a major role and is not under conscious control. We are, therefore, liable to be individually and collectively specialized in our problem solving and subject to difficulties in situations involving increasing creativity and change. However, there is also good news in this discussion. Conscious thinking allows us to choose and embark upon new directions; it makes it possible to fight our habits. We will discuss problem solving habits in more detail in Chapters 4 and 6, since a better understanding of them results in considerable insight into the management of creativity. However, first we will spend some time examining the machinery of problem solving — the brain and the nervous system. By examining it in some detail, we will gain more understanding not only of the problem solving process and inhibitions to increasing creativity and responsiveness to change but also of the need for the "perspiration" mentioned in Chapter 1.

3

The Machinery of
Thinking

In order to drive a car well, we need to know its capabilities: how does it turn, accelerate, and decelerate at different speeds, when does it lose traction on wet pavement, under what conditions does it like to be in which gear, and so on. We do not necessarily need to understand the details of the machinery well enough to do major repairs, but it is helpful to know enough about the machinery to have a sense of the strengths and limitations of the overall system. The brain and nervous system are the machinery that we use to solve problems. We should have a similar understanding of them. Their characteristics give us insight into our strengths and limitations. Their mechanisms explain our habitual nature. The efficiency of their usual processes gives us a better understanding of unusual processes — creativity and change.

We are in an age in which rapid progress is being made in understanding the brain and nervous system. This is due to a number of reasons, including rapid progress in microbiology, advances in medical instrumentation, and the tremendous effort being expended in the field of computer science. The brain is not a computer anymore than the computer is a brain. However, they resemble each other. They each consist of a large number of simple elements and perform certain functions in a similar way. The computer is probably the best analog to a brain that has come along. Certainly attempting to understand the potentials of the computer has motivated brain research and study of the processes that occur in the brain.

I find this research fascinating and important to the understanding of creativity and response to change. When I first became exposed to creativity theory, it was based upon Freudian, behavioral, and humanistic psychology. The keys to managing creativity and change were emotional and cultural. This viewpoint is still valid and will be examined in detail later in this book. However, the more cognitive approach resulting from an understanding of the brain and nervous system gives us additional keys.

Considering the mind from the viewpoint of the biologist and the cognitive scientist sidesteps an old question, namely, Is the mind matter? Is it only three pounds of meat? Is it merely biological material consisting of cells and acting through electrochemical processes or is it more? Does it impinge upon transcendental issues? Are there concepts of higher intelligence, soul, and a universal being involved? These questions have been pondered with delight by philosophers for hundreds of years. The issue of whether the mind is matter is a highly charged one and, should you bring it up at a lively party, you may destroy the party since those who take opposite sides of the debate differ greatly on questions having to do with personal philosophy, faith, and self-identity.

THE MIND AS MACHINERY

In this chapter we will view the mind as brain and nervous system (machinery). Follow patiently, please, even if you think that we give the mechanics of the brain too much credit for the human condition. Considering the mind as machinery results in certain insights into the way we solve problems. We can more clearly see that, although marvelous, the brain and the senses are limited as to their capabilities, and that we solve problems in ways that are consistent with these limitations. Such an approach causes us to better understand reasons for inhibitions to creativity and change, and makes us better understand the way we, our friends, and our colleagues act in new situations. It also results in insights valuable in the management of creativity and change.

It gives one an eerie feeling to view a brain during surgery or to hold a dead brain in one's hands. It becomes more difficult to consider it omniscient and easier to believe that it is a limited machine. If you do not have access to a medical school, you can approximate this feeling by visiting your local butcher shop, buying an animal brain, taking it home, slicing it into pieces, and examining it before you cook it. Interestingly, the brain consists of only two types of cells: neurons and glial (for glue) cells. The latter were once thought to merely "glue" the neurons together, but now we know that their function is much more complex. They are the intermediaries between the body and the neurons, the carriers of nourishment and waste, and the insulators between the neurons. There are more glial cells in the brain than neurons, but even though their function is complex, it is not as important as that of the neuron.

It is the neuron that is the major actor in the brain and nervous system. From the nature of this cell, we can infer quite a bit about the detailed mechanics of our brain and nervous system. Neurons come in different types and shapes. There are sensory neurons, which convey impulses from sense receptors to the rest of the nervous system; motor neurons, which allow the nervous systems to control the muscles; and interneurons, which convey signals from neuron to neuron. Figure 3-1 shows neurons in the brain.

Neurons consist first of all of a cell body that is responsible for the physiological tasks associated with survival of the cell. This cell body, in addition to worrying about general housekeeping, manufactures chemicals called *transmitters*, which are essential to the functioning of the cell. The cell body has fine extensions called *dendrites* and a tail called an *axon*, which may range in length from infinitesimal (in the brain) to several feet (in the spinal cord). The axon terminates in a number of branches, each ending in a *transmitter button*.

The neuron receives incoming signals, integrates them, and sends a corresponding signal down its axon to other cells via the transmitter buttons. Input signals are received either on the dendrites or the cell body itself. They are received in the form of transmitter chemicals, which can either excite the cell or inhibit it. Should one type predominate to a "threshold" level, a signal is sent. In order to do this, the cell body briefly changes the permeability of its membrane wall, allowing a flow of electrically charged particles (ions) across it. This creates a relative electrical charge in the cell (the action potential), which then travels down the axon to the tip.

However, for all of its electrochemical sophistication, the neuron plays a simple game. The speed of the signal in the axon ranges between 1 and 250 miles per hour, depending on the thickness of the axon and other factors. Notice how slow this is compared to the speed of an electrical signal in a wire (186,000 miles per second). When this signal reaches a terminal button, a transmitter chemical then becomes an input to another neuron. In order to reach the other cell, it must travel across a tiny gap called a *synapse*.

FIGURE 3-1　Neurons in the Brain

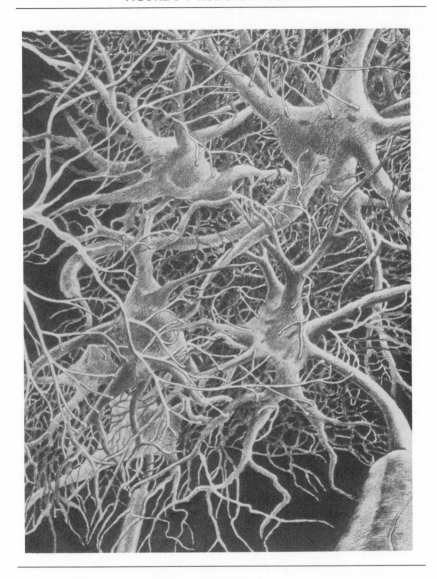

The signal that travels along the neuron is a pulse of fixed intensity. Should the incoming signal increase in intensity, pulses are transmitted more rapidly, but they remain at the same intensity. After a pulse travels through the neuron, a recovery time of approximately 1/1,000 of a second is necessary before the cell recovers sufficiently to send another. A neuron is therefore limited to a signal frequency of approximately 1,000 cycles per second. In the brain, a particular neuron may receive inputs from thousands of other neurons and signal thousands in turn.

There are between 10^{10} and 10^{12} neurons in the brain itself. We will use 10^{11} as the number for this discussion. This is a large number (100,000,000,000). About one-half of the neurons are in the cerebral cortex, which has the greatest density. If we assume that each neuron is connected to 1,000 others, we have 10^{14} (100,000,000,000,000) synapses. Let us imagine a computerlike situation in which each synapse could be "on" or "off." This means that the brain would be capable of $2^{10^{14}}$ different states. This is not the way the brain works, or should work, but this is a truly large number. So large, indeed, that knowing what we know about electrical information processing machinery, we can gain some reassurance that a brain made up of a large number of simple elements (neurons) could be capable of incredibly rich functioning. However, these numbers are not infinite and, if we take into account the slowness of signal movement, the redundancy needed to learn new operations and perform parallel processing, and the allocation of neurons to fixed circuits, we realize that the brain is, in fact, limited. Looked at as a machine, it is indescribably wonderful. However, like any machine, it has limits and therefore causes us to act in certain ways.

LIMITS TO THE MACHINE

We can get a feeling for limitations in the functioning of the brain by performing a few exercises. Later in this book we will discuss what some psychologists call *short-term memory*. It is that part of memory that easily holds information for a short period of time. It is extremely important to us. However, let us experiment with its limitations, since short-term memory is a familiar mental process and you may never have thought about how limited it is.

EXERCISE

Read each of the following sequences of numbers to yourself evenly and carefully. Then, immediately after each sequence, close your eyes and repeat the numbers to yourself.

$$7 \quad 4 \quad 9 \quad 5 \quad 2 \quad 8$$
$$5 \quad 8 \quad 3 \quad 6 \quad 1 \quad 4 \quad 9 \quad 0 \quad 2$$
$$8 \quad 3 \quad 9 \quad 4 \quad 1 \quad 6 \quad 0 \quad 2 \quad 5 \quad 7 \quad 3 \quad 0$$

You probably noticed several things. If you read the numbers evenly, the initial sequence (six digits) was relatively easy to recall. The next sequence was much more difficult, and the last was almost impossible. After a mere doubling of information, from a paltry six digits to a mere twelve, we seem to have reached the limit of short-term memory. In fact, there is a classic psychology article that refers to the magic number seven plus or minus two as the number of items that can be held in a short-term memory.

You might also find this limitation annoying. We should be able easily to remember more than seven digits with our short-term memory. This limit is typical of many thinking limits because we have learned to live with it, are not conscious of it, and are surprised when we are forced to confront it. I can give you a situation that will make you realize that you understand the limit. Imagine that you are in a city trying to call an out-of-state number from a phone booth with no directory, no pencil, and no credit card. You insert the coins, dial the information operator, and are given the area code and the number. This is a sequence of ten digits. You repeat the sequence to yourself (a technique used to keep things in short-term memory) while hanging up, retrieving the coins, and dialing it. At the time the ringing begins, you stop repeating the sequence. Should the ringing turn into a busy signal, where are you? Probably with an overstretched short-term memory and the need to return to the operator. Obviously, we are not always sensitive to this limitation. If we were, we wouldn't be messing around with uncoded nine-digit zip codes.

You may also have noticed that short-term memory is severely limited in time. Unless you have a photographic memory you can't recall the nine-digit number in the preceding exercise without looking back at it. During the exercise you may have noticed that you tended to read the digits to yourself in groups rather than evenly. That process is called chunking, and it is an automatic part of our remembering process, since the memory is almost as willing to hold seven chunks of data as it is seven digits. If you grouped the twelve digits into four complex three-digit numbers, for instance, you found the information much easier to hold. More about such things later. For now, we are mostly interested in short-term memory as a demonstration of a thinking limit.

As we mentioned in the last chapter, the brain is also limited in speed. Here is an opportunity to experience this.

In your mind, figure out how many capital letters of the English alphabet have curved lines in them. See how rapidly you can figure this out.

This exercise should have brought you up against a frustrating limit to the speed at which conscious thought can occur. You were not much faster than a carousel projector, since you almost had to literally "look" at each letter. If you do not think that your mind is limited to something approaching the speed of life, see if you can imagine a tennis match being played at 1,000 times normal speed. How about 100 times? 10 times? 4 times? Once again this experience may be frustrating since we assume that we can think much faster than we live. Incidentally, there are eleven capitals in the alphabet with curved lines in them.

As we also saw in the last chapter, your conscious mind is limited as to how many things it can do at once. You know all sorts of clever strategies to make it appear that you can do several things at once, but in actuality you are limited. For instance, you would find that you could only count by sevens and at the same time count backwards from one hundred by threes if you alternated. You would also find it difficult to do much else in the way of thinking while you were occupied at this task.

PROGRAMMING OF THE BRAIN

Neurons do not reproduce or replace themselves, so we are born with our full complement of neurons. As you are aware, the "blueprint" for our biological development is contained in our genes, which are in turn contained in the first single fertilized cell in the womb of our mothers. As this cell divides, each resulting cell has a complete copy of the genes of our parent cell, and this continues throughout our development. This information allows a particular cell to be a kidney cell, a toenail cell, or a brain cell, and to take its particular place and role in the developing organism. The genes obviously carry a tremendous amount of information for an individual. However, they do not carry nearly enough information to determine completely the precise interconnection of all the neurons in the brain. The majority of the neuronal connections arise through some other process. What process? Good question.

One of the more active areas of research these days is the attempt to understand the functional and anatomical changes that occur within neuronal circuits as a result of an organism's experience. This phenomenon is called plasticity. It is easy to believe that some neuronal circuitry is hard-wired by the genes very early in our development, since we need some functions, such as heartbeat and breathing, early. Other functions, such as our propensity to develop languages of similar forms, are undoubtedly at least influenced by the genes. Even some behavior characteristics that seem predominant in particular families may have a genetically determined component. However, much of our behavior and intellectual skill and essentially all of our knowledge is learned, and mechanisms must exist to allow this to happen. Our genes did not give us the knowledge that the capital of the U.S. is Washington D.C.

If we thought the brain was merely a sophisticated computer, we might think that the mechanism of plasticity was entirely electromagnetic, as it is in the memory of the computer on which I composed these pages. However, the consensus of the biological community is that much more is happening in the brain than electrical signals; that, in fact, as we live chemical and physical changes take place within the brain that alter its actions. Biologists, for instance, feel that there is physical change accompanying memory. As argument, they point to the incredible persistence of some memories (early childhood memories last vividly until death) and to the fact that the human body can be cooled to the point where brain waves are severely decreased and then brought back to normal temperature with intact memory. In a sense, the plug can be pulled on the computer and yet the memory remains when the plug is put back into the wall.

It is suspected that the material undergoing these changes is in the synapses. The mechanism is not yet entirely understood, although quite a bit is known or suspected about it. For instance, there are apparently periods of life when plasticity is at a maximum. Brain growth in animals, including humans, seems to correlate with times in which much change is occurring in neuronal structure. As an example, after birth the human baby begins the process of finally determining the visual cortex. This happens after a week or so for the rat, who is born blind with eyes closed. There are large spurts of growth in the human brain at birth and in the rat brain a week or so later. Interconnects are being formed and existing interconnects are being affected. The interconnects are obviously being affected by experience.

This dependence of plasticity on age and experience probably explains many differences between children and adults. It may have something to do with the ability of very young children to learn a second language with no particular accent, whereas adults find it increasingly difficult to do so. It no doubt explains the unusual ability of children below the age of five or so to relearn functions in other portions of their brain after damage has occurred. Adults have this ability to a much lesser degree. Developmental psychology.is full of references to the age of five. In the younger human, the synaptic framework obviously is capable of great change.

How about the older human — that creature of mature grace and beauty and enviable worldliness? Obviously, plasticity is still with us. We still learn. We acquire new knowledge, skills, and even attitudes as we age. A famous quote states: "The young man who is not a liberal has no heart — the old man who is not a conservative has no mind." The learning of tennis after football or lawn-bowling after tennis shows plasticity. In fact, short of such factors as Alzheimer's disease, there is no evidence that we lose our ability to make new connections. There seem to be certain phenomena, such as weakening of recent memory, that accompany aging, but no physical reason has been found. Possibly we are merely overfilling our files. We lose neurons every day of our life, but as we have seen, we begin with a very large number.

Old dogs can learn new tricks. However, old problem-solving dogs must also realize that much of their knowledge, attitudes, and abilities are wired in — controlled by neuronal networks that have physically and chemically been determined by experience. Old dogs must also understand that there is difficulty associated with learning new tricks. I frequently find successful older professionals decrying their seeming inability to learn new techniques, such as use of the computer. In fact, they are capable of learning such things as easily as they ever were, they are just no longer willing to spend the necessary time and effort. Think of the time we have spent learning mathematics in school. If we were to learn similar material now it would obviously take as long. Would we spend that amount of time and effort now? What we know about thinking limitations and the mechanisms of plasticity leads us to a better understanding of the need for habit in problem solving and gives us more insight into the difficulty of creativity and change.

FUNCTIONAL SPECIALIZATION

Enough on composition and mechanisms. Let us now discuss functional specialization in the brain. By that we mean the extent to which brain function is localized in different areas. There are many theories, all of which lead to the conclusion that localization might result in biases and other limits in problem solving. Many of these theories are described in the fascinating book *Maps of the Mind*, by Charles Hampden-Turner. Figure 3-2 is a drawing of a human brain showing areas of specialization. Two models of functional specialization that are often encountered these days are the "triune brain" concept of Paul MacLean, popularized in Carl Sagan's Pulitzer-prize-winning book *Dragons of Eden*, and the "split-brain" model that underlies discussions of "right-brain" and "left-brain" thinking. In MacLean's theory, each of three concentric parts of the human brain contribute to human behavior in a different way. At the base of the brain is the

FIGURE 3-2 A Functional Map of the Human Brain

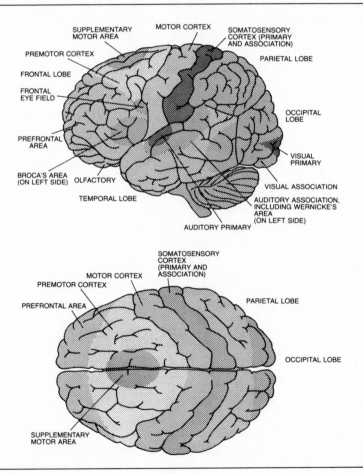

R-complex. (The *R* stands for reptile.) This is the human hindbrain and is similar to the dominant portions of the reptile brain. According to MacLean, the *R*-complex is responsible for deep behavioral characteristics shared by all beasts. The need for ceremony and hierarchy is perhaps one, as is our desire to return home occasionally (reptiles, for instance, return home to lay their eggs). The *R*-complex is beneath conscious communication and causes primitive urges that we must answer.

Over the hindbrain we find the limbic system, which although not major in reptiles, does show up in lower mammals. According to the triune brain concept, the limbic system is the source of emotional behavior having to do with reproduction and survival of the species. It is the source of love and passion, which one expects more from a puppy than from a turtle. It is easier to communicate with consciously, but not completely controllable by logic. We continue to do things in the name of love that do not always appear to be wise.

The third component of MacLean's three-part brain is the cortex. This is unique to "higher" animals and reaches its zenith in humans. It is capable of argument and communication and is accessible to the psychotherapist. By explaining behavior in terms of the *R*-complex, the limbic system, and the cerebral cortex, MacLean has produced a rather elegant, if oversimplified, model of the brain that juxtaposes anatomy and behavior. It is not accepted by either biologists or psychologists, but gives us interesting insights. We would like to think that we are primarily logical, thinking beings (cortex). However, we act as though there is quite a bit of *R*-complex and limbic system involved. It is beneficial to realize how much of our behavior and decision making are rooted in deeper, more habitual bases than the conscious thought that resides in our cortex. Simple models such as that of MacLean give us a framework to think about such things.

There is an interesting similarity in various models of the mind in that many of them make use either of two parts in opposition (left, right) or three parts of increasingly "human" character (id, ego, superego). The majority of models contain an unconscious portion that is not easily controllable by the portion that we usually think of as being in control. It is useful to analyze creativity and change in light of these models, since our actions are not always consistent with our desires and self-images.

For another example of functional specialization that leads us to conjecture about limits, let us examine the "left-brain/right-brain" model. Quite a bit of attention has been given to this during the past few years. The split-brain model has historically lurked in the background of many cultures. "Right-handed thinking" has been generally associated with logic, mathematics, language, judgment, and force (adroit, dextrous). Similarly, "left-handed thinking" has been associated with intuition, imagery, and fantasy (sinister, leftist). Beginning in the 1960s, a series of remarkable experiments by Roger Sperry and his group at the California Institute of Technology and Michael Gazzaninga and his colleagues at the Huntington Memorial Hospital in Pasadena indicated that if the right and left hemispheres of the cortex are separated by severing the corpus callosum, they will function differently. Taking into account that the right hand is controlled by the left side of the brain and that the left hand is controlled by the right side, the conclusions support the folklore. The left side of the brain is concerned with speech and logic; the right with imagery.

In one of the experiments, a human subject whose corpus callosum had been severed surgically in an epilepsy procedure was shown pictures in such a way that the images reached either the right or left hemisphere of her brain. When she was shown a picture of a nude woman so that it reached her left hemisphere, she laughed and described it correctly. When the same picture was later presented to the right hemisphere, she said that she saw nothing, but immediately afterward began to chuckle. When asked what was funny, she said, "I don't know . . . nothing . . . oh — that funny machine." Her left hemisphere, the verbal one, had correctly identified the image and responded emotionally. Her right hemisphere had also obviously identified the image, since it had responded emotionally, but could not identify it in words.

The split-brain model, although again an elegant one based on a combination of physiology and behavior, is also controversial. It certainly is consistent with our personal experience. We have no trouble accusing schools of emphasizing left-brain material and ignoring the right brain. Similarly, we have no trouble speaking of computer zealots as being overly left brain. However, the experiments were performed with subjects in which the corpus callosum had been severed. Portions of complicated systems do not act the same when isolated as they do when interconnected. Split brain theory also seems inconsistent with highly coordinated intellectual acts such as those involved with the composition, performance, and appreciation of music. Finally, it is of less importance to those involved in therapy and therefore viewed suspiciously by the psychiatric community. Therapists tend to be interested in the "whole" person. However, for us it is an interesting theory because it suggests to us that our thinking and problem solving is not all logical, verbal, and conscious, but contains elements more sinister (and useful) as well.

We have suggested that the brain is limited in process and by functional specialization. It should be obvious that this is important to the management of creativity and change. We are painting a mechanistic picture of the problem-solving machinery. The brain is obviously wonderful, but not omniscient. With its limits and electro-chemical nature, it is not too hard to believe that it makes heavy use of programming. It would also make sense for it to be programmed to operate most efficiently for usual business, since we spend the majority of our time engaged in usual business.

SENSING INFORMATION

The brain is the processor and the senses are the source of the input to our brain. All of the information that we use in problem solving and, in fact, in living, comes to us initially through our senses. Sensing is accomplished by the sensors, the nervous system, and the brain acting as a unit. It involves memory and is affected by emotional and cultural factors. If we fail to hear the phone ringing at a party, it is difficult to say whether the ear did not detect it or whether the brain merely did not attend to it. To the extent that our senses limit or otherwise affect the information we receive from the world, they affect our problem-solving ability. Similarly, the processing of this information, whether it is to be used directly or stored in memory, plays a direct role in our thinking.

Our senses, like our brains, are limited. One of our most common errors is to assume that our model of the world is reality. It is our personal reality, but it does not necessarily correspond to nature. It is merely a model made from the information to which our particular sensors are sensitive after this information is processed by our brain. Your model is not the same model as that of the person next to you, since not only is that person's brain filled with different information and procedures, but his or her sensors differ from yours in sensitivity.

A good example of this difference is color blindness, which is present to some extent in approximately 8 percent of males. It is safe to say that everyone knows someone who has some color blindness. However, the subject seldom arises in dealings between people. Each person has a workable model of the world and, in fact, would have trouble imaging the visual model of the other. Many people who are color-blind do not discover it until they are fairly old, since their model seems totally complete to them. (It is the only one they have.) Yet people who are not color-blind would view the loss of color sensitivity as a tragedy.

Limitations of the senses are consistent with a finite brain. It would simply not make sense for us to completely process all of the information that impinges upon us in life. It might be fun to be able to see infrared, ultraviolet, x, and the other bands in the electromagnetic spectrum and, in fact, many of these frequencies outside of the visual range are useful to us, but our brain would at some point be overwhelmed by information. We have evolved in a way so that we are sensitive only to the information that is pertinent to us.

Sensory limitations trip us up in two ways. First of all, they give us problem-solving information that is incomplete. Second, they lead to biases in our problem solving based on biases in information. As an example, we tend to rely more heavily on visual information than on information from our other senses. This may cause us to miss important inputs.

The senses are usually grouped in the following categories:

vision:	sight
hearing:	sound
movement:	vestibular (orientation)
	kinesthetic (body configuration)
skin:	pressure, hot-cold, pain
chemical:	taste, smell
organic:	state of body (hunger, sexual satiation, etc.)
time:	passage of time

The first five categories have specific sensors to detect the pertinent information and have certain characteristics in common. They have sensitivity ranges, or bandwidths, which cause them to detect certain types of intensities and frequencies of information and not others. A term that is often encountered when studying the senses is *threshold*, which refers to the level of signal necessary before the sensor recognizes that something is happening. Thresholds are very low for traditional signals (touch: you can feel the wing of a fly falling on your cheek from a distance of one centimeter; smell: you can detect one drop of perfume diffused in the entire volume of a six-room apartment) and very high for nontraditional signals (high-frequency sound: you can't hear it at a frequency above 20,000 hertz). The senses tend to be more sensitive to changes in information than to common input. In fact, the senses tend to accommodate to constant signals over time. Sensitivity to change varies from sense to sense (for example, a change in sound pitch of 1/133 of the original level can be detected, but salinity must be increased by 1/5 before a difference can be noticed). In general, there is a correlation between sensitivity and survival value. Salinity is a general measure of environmental interest and it is important to detect major shifts. Sight and hearing, on the other hand, detect instantaneous events that could immediately spell danger.

Finally, the first five senses are integrated. Our appreciation of food depends upon sight, smell, taste, and, perhaps, feel and sound. Head position is inherent in locating the source of a sound, and a number of our senses may be needed to ascertain whether it is our train that is moving or the one on the next track.

The last two sense categories, the organic and time senses, are not as well understood as the first five. However, they are included in the list because of their importance in problem solving. Time is usually a factor, as is the state of the body. Let us discuss a few of these senses in a little more detail in order to better understand the limitations that our senses place on problem solving. Vision will be examined as an example of the way in which we interpret reality; the skin senses as an indication of how we take our senses for granted; the chemical senses as an indication of difficulty in communicating useful information from our senses; and, finally, the organic and time senses will be discussed because of their pertinence to problem solving.

Vision is perhaps our most important sense. It not only requires a large amount of our nervous tissue and brain for its functions, but also plays a key role in the problems of day-to-day living. Vision is often dominant over our other senses when conflicting information is received. In one psychology experiment that showed this dominance, a square, whose outline showed through a cloth, was felt by experimental subjects at the same time they viewed the outline through a distorting lens that made it appear rectangular. They concluded that it was rectangular.

The wavelength of the energy in the electromagnetic spectrum varies over some 22 orders of magnitude. However, the visible range varies only over two. There are evolutionary as well as practical reasons for the visible spectrum being where it is. Ultraviolet and infrared frequencies (those just outside the visible range at the high and low end) do not penetrate over a meter or two of water. Therefore, if we evolved from creatures that lived beneath the seas, our blindness to ultraviolet and infrared frequencies makes sense. However, these frequencies are useful to us, as is demonstrated by our manufacture of detectors to "see" them. Reality obviously includes them. The first message, therefore, is our blindness to the majority of the electromagnetic spectrum. The eye also has a blind spot where the optic nerve fibers collect. If you have never been aware of this, look at Figure 3-3.

FIGURE 3-3 The Blind Spot

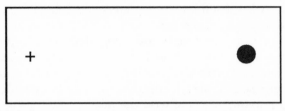

Close the left eye and fixate the right eye on the cross. Slowly move the page back and forth from the eye between 5 and 15 inches until the position is reached at which the spot disappears. The spot is then falling on the region of the retina where the nerve fibers group together and leave the eye.

As you also may remember from your high school biology class, our eye is more sensitive to light in the peripheral regions of the retina, although acuity is lower. That is why one is better off using peripheral vision when illumination is low. The maximum acuity is in the *fovea*, or central region of the retina, which is why we look directly "at" an object we want to see well if illumination permits. Like other predators, we have binocular vision, giving us the ability to judge distances. However, in order to do so, we have sacrificed field of view. The rabbit, like other animals of prey, has little binocular vision but is able to boast of field of view approaching 360 degrees.

Our eye is not good at judging illumination levels, as we could guess from the light meters on our cameras. Our eyes also take a significant time to adapt to a quick change in illumination. This is presumably because we evolved in natural lighting instead of artificial illumination. When moving from a well lit to a poorly lit environment, full adaptation requires up to half an hour. Our eye also has a finite speed of response to image change. After a stimulus has been removed, an image remains for a short period of time. This phenomenon allows us to enjoy motion pictures, which are a series of still images. However, it prevents us from being able to see specific events that occur at a rate of over 15 per second.

The eye must also move. The retina adapts to a fixed image. Experiments have been performed in which an image is projected on a fixed position on the retina and within a few seconds, the subjects no longer detect the image. There are two types of movements — pursuit movements, which are the smooth movements our eyes employ to track a target, and *saccades*, which are very rapid movements from one place to the other. These are very fast (two or three per second) and are used to search the visual field. Vision is impaired during these movements (which occupy approximately 10 percent of viewing time) but the movements are so fast that we are not aware of it.

To summarize, the eye, although a marvel, is blind outside of the visual spectrum, limited in acuity, light adaptation, and response time. The eyes search a visual field with continual small movements, which are functions of personal priorities, the task as understood, and personality. Large variations exist between individuals with respect to optical characteristics. We hardly need mention acuity differences due to common sight disorders such as astigmatism, nearsightedness, and farsightedness. There are also differences in night vision and dark adaptation, color sensitivity, and ability to view the far edges of the visible spectrum.

There are still more limitations and differences because of the major involvement of the brain in interpreting the signals from the eyes. The brain automatically compensates for traditional situations where visual confusion could occur. For instance, if I walk away from you, the image that I cast on your retina decreases in size. However, you do not think I am shrinking. Your brain compensates by using its knowledge of perspective. However, this knowledge can cause trouble. Optical illusions are often examples of this, as are the maddening aspects of many prints by M. C. Escher (see Figure 3-4).

To witness one of the more popular illusions, draw two vertical lines approximately three inches long and approximately one inch apart that are parallel and equal in length. Now draw arrowheads on both ends of one of the lines (a *V* approximately one inch long facing inward) and reversed arrowheads on both ends of the other (a *V* approximately one inch long facing outward). What happens? The beauty of this illusion (Müller-Lyer illusion) is that even though you drew the lines the same length, one line ended up seeming longer than the other.

One explanation for this illusion is that the line with the arrowheads looks like the near corner of a building, and the one with the reversed arrowheads resembles the far corner of a building. Your brain knows that more distant objects subtend a smaller angle on the retina. Therefore, if two lines subtend the same angle and one is farther away (the far corner), that corner must be taller (see Figure 3-5). The line, therefore, appears longer. This is typical of explanations for the success of optical illusions. They are successful because powerful programs exist in the mind to reduce usual data. When the mind encounters unusual data, the programs will act anyway and an apparently distorted reality will occur. This use of programs not

FIGURE 3-4 M. C. Escher, *Other World*, 1947, wood engraving

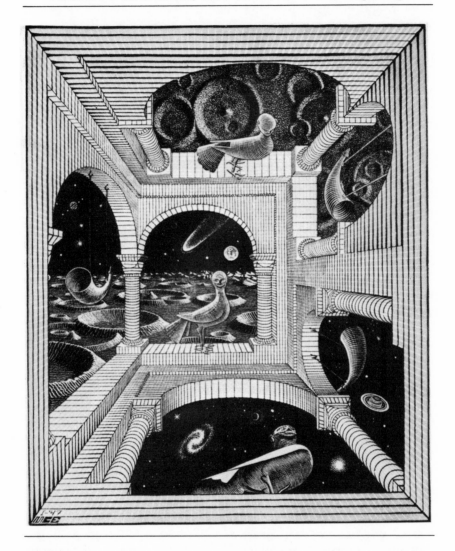

only allows us to deal with a three-dimensional world, but also allows us to operate on less than perfect data. What is the object in Figure 3-6, for instance? Your mind has no trouble detecting a person on a horse, even though the information is sparse. Figures 3-7 and 3-8 also allow you to think about what your visual senses do to your information gathering. Once again, you should suspect that habits exist in your problem-solving process in order to augment your limited visual sense.

FIGURE 3-5 The Müller-Lyer Illusion

FIGURE 3-6 A Perceptual Problem

Similar statements can be made about the other sense groups. Although marvelous, they do not deliver "reality" to us and have all manner of limitations and idiosyncrasies. In addition, our conscious mind is often oblivious to input from many of our sensors. We can gain an appreciation of this by examining the haptic, or skin, senses. This group is my favorite, since the skin is very impressive and yet given so little credit. The skin is a large and complex organ. It measures approximately 1.75 square meters (3,000 square inches) for an average-size male. It shields us from outside objects and energies,

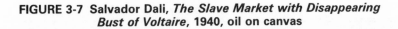

FIGURE 3-7 Salvador Dali, *The Slave Market with Disappearing Bust of Voltaire*, 1940, oil on canvas

actively helps control our temperature, holds in vital fluids, plays a role in regulating blood flow, and makes us more attractive to our friends. In addition, the skin detects various incoming signals of great importance in protecting us from danger and in sensing the nature of our environment. Specifically, the skin is sensitive to pressure, temperature, and pain. These signals are often integrated — for example, when we hold onto an ice cube for too long. Much of our model of ourselves also comes from the skin — the state of our environment, our comfort, our physical configuration, and whether we are about to be harmed by something we have contacted. Even though the skin is not usually given a great deal of credit for providing information, it is possible to do quite well in many situations when other senses are not helping much (for example, in making one's way through a pitch-black and silent landscape — try it some moonless night).

The skin contains an array of sensors that transmit the state of the local environment to the brain. These signals are by no means uniform. For instance, sensitivity to pressure ranges widely over the body. A single filament of nylon requires 350 milligrams of pressure

FIGURE 3-8 Another Perceptual Problem

for detection on the male big toe but only 5 milligrams on the sensitive parts of the face. There is also large variation on the skin's ability to differentiate two pressure points. Points a few millimeters apart can be detected as separate on the finger, while on the calf a spacing of 40 millimeters or more is necessary before the two can be detected. Try it on your own skin.

Our ability to sense temperature is even more complicated. We are capable of detecting changes in skin temperature from a temperature called physiological zero. However, physiological zero varies over the body and is a function of previous adaptation. This can be demonstrated by submerging one hand in water at 40 degrees C.

and the other in water at 20 degrees C. Remove both hands and submerge them in water at 33 degrees C. The new bath will feel warm to the hand that was in the colder water and cool to the hand that was in the warmer. The skin is not a particularly good measurement device for absolute temperature. Instead, it measures deviation. We are more sensitive to increases in temperature if we have adapted to high temperature and more sensitive to decreases if we have adapted to low. This is convenient because, in order to avoid damage to ourselves, we should be more sensitive to extreme temperatures.

Pain is perhaps the most complex of the quantities sensed by the skin. Even more than temperature, our perception of pain is a function of many things. It is obvious that high-level decisions are involved in some aspects of pain, since it has been well documented that in certain situations our pain is not as debilitating as in others. Pain is not only a function of information to the sensors but also of our overall physical and psychological state.

If we now think about what we have said concerning the skin, we can conclude that it, too, follows our generalizations for the senses. A great many things go on in the skin that contribute to our model of the world. However, we are not generally aware of the mechanics nor are we generally aware of the nature of the "readings" we get from our sensors. We are merely aware of our final model of the world. We get less information from constant situations than from changing ones, and our information is a function of the state of any situation. The information we receive tends to be biased toward physical survival and is efficient in that less data is available about characteristics of our world that are not critical in our living. The skin "sorts" information in order to serve us well in the context of the finite characteristics of our brain and nervous system. Unfortunately, the sorting is biased more toward physical survival at an earlier time than toward the problem-solving environment in which most of us presently live.

It is of interest to consider the chemical senses for yet a different reason. The message concerning their limitations is similar. The senses that let us blend Scotch, appreciate gourmet cuisine, become aroused by someone of the opposite sex, and appreciate the smell of a rose are not as omnipotent as we might think. They are more important in lower forms of life both to determine the safety of the environment and for activities leading to the satisfaction of basic needs such as hunger and procreation. Certainly our sense of smell is not as impressive as that of our dog. Nor is our ability to detect changes in taste as good as that of the catfish. Not all of our chemical sensors are in the nose and mouth. We can detect strong acids on the skin, onion fumes in the eyes, and alcohol in the gastrointestinal tract. However, these far-ranging sensors act as warning systems rather than sources of data in problem solving. The sensors in the nose and mouth are more likely to be directly involved.

The chemical senses are particularly interesting in the context of this book in that they give us an example of our surprisingly poor ability to communicate some of our important sensory information. It is fairly simple, for instance, for me to describe a visual image in words without using direct names such that you can identify it. Suppose, for instance, that I tell you that I am imagining a machine with a framework made of tubing, a spoked wheel at either end, one of which can be steered by means of a bent pipe and the other of which can be turned by means of a chain, and a leather device on the top on which to sit. You could quite rapidly guess what I was describing. Now try the following;

E X E R C I S E

Find a partner. Each of you should think of a smell that is vivid to you. Now take turns describing the smell you chose to each other, avoiding the use of direct names ("like a flower," "like brie cheese," etc.). Do the same with a taste.

What do you conclude? Most people find this almost impossibly difficult. We share an experience (such as the smell of a rose) that we cannot describe in words. Once again, this is perhaps at odds with our self-image. We are, after all, highly articulate. Yet we have a surprising lack of language with which to describe information from the chemical sensors. We find that even those who study the chemical senses have difficulty in agreeing on language to describe them. We agree that the four sensations of bitter, sour, salt, and sweet are all that the taste sensors can detect, but the sensation depends upon the recent history of the sensor, since tastes interact and the sensors rapidly adapt. It also depends upon factors such as the age, health, and psychological set of the individual.

Smell is more complicated. It is one of the most primitive senses. The nerves from the sensors connect directly to the higher cortical regions. Smell is probably the sense most capable of instantly evoking strong emotions and memories. I once was in love with a girl who liked and wore gardenias. Gardenias still cause me to remember her even though 35 years have passed. However, like the other senses, smell is easily confused. Like taste, the sensors adapt quickly and the sensation is a function of recent past history, health, and psychological set of the individual.

There is less agreement on the basic components of the sensation of smell. A simple model does not exist. One attempt places fragrant, ethereal, putrid, burned, spicy, and resinous at the corners of a three-sided prism. I shall never forget, after acquiring a background in sophisticated optical and electromechanical detectors in the aerospace business, my delight on encountering the odorimeter, an instrument used to measure the intensity and character of smells. It fit over the human nose and allowed the alternation of the subject smell with standard smells. It is not only undignified, it was fairly useless because of the difficulty in interpolating between subject and standard smells, the adaptation of the nose, and the occasional presence of detractions such as the common cold.

What can we say of the organic senses and the time sense? They are the more mysterious of the senses, since we cannot locate simple sensors to analyze. The organic sense tells you whether you are healthy, whether you are hungry or thirsty, whether you are sleepy, and whether you are sexually sated. What does this have to do with problem solving? Think a bit about the cues that you use to steer your way through the solution of a complicated problem. In particular, how do you decide between alternate interim answers. Certainly you can try to analyze their potential. You can ask for the advice of others. But what about the role played by feelings? Don't you have feelings of "upness" when you are going in a direction where light may exist at the end of the tunnel and depression when you are not? One of the more popular quotes in the creativity literature is Albert Einstein's answer to a query from Jaque Hadamard about his problem-solving method: "The words or the language, as they are written or spoken, do not seem to play any role in my mechanism of thought. The psychical entities which seem to serve as elements in thought are certain signs and more or less clear images which can be 'voluntarily' reproduced and combined. . . . The above mentioned elements are, in my case, of visual and some of muscular type."

What would you guess those muscular elements are? I doubt if Einstein actually used his muscle fibers in his logic. He was rather referring to the feeling that he used to navigate his way through work. How does this feeling reach the mind? Undoubtedly, it does so through the organic senses. In a similar manner, you undoubtedly have noticed differences in your sleepiness, the state of your stomach, and in your sex drive as you work on problems. Perhaps even conditions such as migraine headaches, lower-back problems, and tachycardia are present. The organic senses are intimately involved in problem solving and send signals of impending success, unacceptable risk, and even unacceptable mediocrity. However, these feelings may be untrustworthy. It may be that you should take the risk even though you may have to spend more time close to a toilet.

Time is also very important in problem solving. It not only is involved in apportioning effort toward a deadline, but also plays a role in states of panic and lethargy. As you no doubt realize, we operate under two types of time: clock and psychological. We are all familiar with clock time, since we can watch it on our wrist and use it to fill our calendars. Psychological time, however, does not follow clock time. It can make an hour in a meeting interminable and an hour with a new love pass very quickly. It can make a pleasurable two-week vacation seem like years while you are living through it and minutes after you return. It can cause you to think that you have known your spouse forever and yet also a very short time. In solving problems, psychological time is responsible for the apparently leisurely pace at the beginning and the mad race at the end. It is once again impressive (you can do an excellent job of keeping track of time without a clock) but limited (you do not live as though you can).

INFORMATION AND PROBLEM SOLVING

In this chapter we have discussed the brain and the senses — the system that gathers and physically processes information. Unfortunately, research on this system has not yet uncovered the fundamental mechanisms of creativity. We do not know why information is sometimes processed in a way that results in new combinations and other times not. We do not know why our emotions welcome some combinations and not others. We are certainly a long way from a creativity pill. However, better understanding of this system gives us valuable insight into the processes of creativity and change.

A mathematician, a physicist, and I are presently developing a rather ambitious and still experimental year-long course in the nature of technology, mathematics, and science for Stanford students majoring in the humanities and sciences. Although these students have a good high school background in technical subjects and high aptitude, they, for a number of reasons, have lost their confidence in and liking for quantitative thinking. It is precisely for this reason that we are developing the course. Our hypothesis, which is turning out to be true, is that the students have developed negative attitudes toward technology, science, and mathematics without ever having been given a chance to examine them. (Clue: they have little to do with high school math courses.) We are, therefore, attempting to operate at a fairly advanced conceptual level.

I have just had the students design small electrically-powered vehicles. The purpose of the project was to allow them to experience some of the thought processes of engineers. I pulled few punches on the project.

For the students it was a highly creative experience, sometimes verging on the traumatic. For me, it was a demonstration of specialized machines (brains and nervous systems) being asked to operate in new ways. The students had to acquire and process new information of a type they were not used to handling. They were used to working verbally, yet designing physical items requires working with imagery. They had been programmed through their course work to think that technical work is based on right answers, and yet there are few right answers in design. They were used to working at the speed at which one can scan written material, not mathematical material. Their R-complexes and limbic systems, if you will, were not pleased with technical material, and mere logic could not easily sway them. Few of them were programmed for the combination of right- and left-brain activity required in design.

It is apparent in any exercise such as this that people prefer to operate in a business-as-usual mode. To ask adults to solve problems in an unusual way is to challenge the machinery of the brain and nervous system. The students eventually did an exceptional job because they are intelligent, motivated, and willing to expend the necessary effort to process the proper information in the correct way. Their vehicle designs were highly creative. As is often the case, they ended up with a strong sense of satisfaction and increased confidence. However, a solid month of highly conscious effort was necessary to overcome the traditional limits of their brains and nervous systems. If I simplified their task at all, it was through continually drawing attention to the fact that conscious effort was normally required in order to travel in new directions and not a sign of stupidity. I also reminded them that intellectual adventures are like all adventures — the pleasure at the end is sometimes enhanced by a bit of agony en route.

If you think about the material in this chapter and then list principles to increase creativity, your list might resemble this one:

1. When solving problems remain aware that the information you have in your mind is not complete and not identical to that of those around you.
2. Be aware that your brain would like to follow a traditional pattern — to simplify your life by applying solutions that have successfully

worked before. Be grateful for that, but suspicious that the creativity you are looking for may not occur automatically.

3. The brain is efficient in business-as-usual situations. It is able to make use of past experience and apply it quickly and unconsciously. However, it may be less efficient in new situations.

4. Conscious effort is both able and necessary to pursue new directions. Perspiration is, in fact, an excellent investment.

This is a pretty good list. As we will later discuss, perhaps the most common inhibition to creativity is our usual reliance upon traditional problem-solving routines and the fantasy that creative problem solving should be easier, rather than more difficult, than producing answers to routine problems.

In these first chapters of this book we are examining mental activity from several perspectives. Our goal is to better understand the nature of problem solving, for it is this understanding that we need to better manage creativity and change. We have talked about conscious and unconscious thinking and the mechanisms of the brain and nervous system. In the next chapter we will begin examining problem solving habits in a more general way. Just as unconscious thinking can best be understood by considering conscious thinking and its limitations, insights to creativity result from a consideration of habitual thinking and what it cannot do.

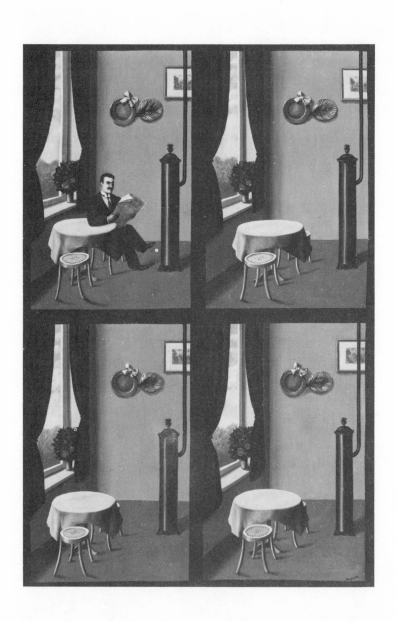

4

Habit and Problem Solving

As we said at the beginning of this book, one essential element of creativity and change is deviance. We do not want to embark upon new directions stupidly. We certainly want to use our knowledge and experience as best we can. However, we are heading into the unknown, and old habits simply may not work. From our discussion of the unconscious and the nature of the brain and nervous system you should have gained an appreciation of some of the reasons for habit. It is worthwhile to spend some time thinking about habits in more detail, because, to the extent that they inhibit creativity and change, we must become clever at modifying or circumventing them.

An example of an intellectual habit, which plagued many of the students mentioned in the last chapter, is reliance on verbal language. The students would engage in frantic discussion about sizes, shapes, details of mechanisms, and other physical features that simply cannot be adequately specified in words. It was not that they did not know how to draw and specify things quantitatively. It was simply that they were used to operating with words; they had a verbal habit that overwhelmed other methods of thinking. It was only necessary to move them into thinking visually and in terms of forms and physical details for extraordinary creativity (for them, deviance) to occur.

Let us begin our discussion by considering physical habits — complicated actions that we have learned to do automatically. Try the following:

E X E R C I S E

1. Clasp your hands in front of you and look at them. Notice which thumb is on top. Unclasp them and reclasp them so that your other thumb is on top. Notice anything?
2. Fold your hands across your chest. Notice that one of your wrists is on top. Unfold them and refold them so that the other wrist is on top. What happened?
3. Take your shoes off. Now put the "wrong" one on first.

These are simple physical habits, but they do remind us that we are programmed, at least physically, in our daily lives. They further show that, through conscious effort, a desire to do something differently, and "instructions" as to what we want to accomplish, we can modify our habits. Our first attempts seem awkward, even wrong. However, with reinforcement, we can learn new programs. As far as physical movement is concerned, any of you who have broken a bone (especially in your dominant hand or arm) have experienced this. You were at first overwhelmed by familiar objects such as pencils, buttons, and toilet paper. However, after a few weeks you were getting along.

How about more complex habits? Think about typing a letter, playing a musical instrument, participating in your favorite sport, or driving a car. These require more conscious attention than clasping your hands, folding your arms, or putting your shoes on. In fact, in each case your consciousness is busy making strategic decisions — What shall I say in my letter? What intonation should this passage have? Will she come to the net and, if so, where should I lob or pass? Where in the world is Cactus Avenue? However, in each case you are also doing much of the activity habitually, or automatically. In fact, if you perform these activities or similar ones, you can remember back to the time when you were "learning" them and realize that complex combinations that at one time were cumbersome and required tremendous conscious effort are now completely unconscious. You now can think of what you want to say and have it appear on the paper or in musical sounds, contemplate a strategy and have it happen on the court, or commute to work in the morning with an almost frightening lack of conscious effort.

How about intellectual efforts? We are not accustomed to using the word *habit* with respect to thinking as much as with physical actions. However, we can reach similar conclusions. As an example, let us consider a basic learned problem solving technique — that of subtraction. Subtraction has been taught at least two different ways in our schools. The two approaches are:

Approach #1

1. Subtract lower number in right-hand column from upper. If lower is numerically larger than upper, add 10 to upper and then subtract. Write difference as right-hand digit of answer.
2. Move one column to left. If 10 was added in preceding step, decrease upper number by one. If lower is numerically larger than upper, add 10 to upper and then subtract. Write difference as next digit of answer and repeat this step until problem is complete.

Approach #2

1. Subtract lower number in right-hand column from upper. If lower is numerically larger than upper, add 10 to upper and then subtract. Write difference as right-hand digit of answer.
2. Move one column to left. If 10 was added in preceding step, increase lower number by one. If lower number is numerically larger than upper, add 10 to upper and then subtract. Write difference as next digit of answer and repeat this step until problem is complete.

As done in the third grade, the problems might look like this:

Approach #1

$$\begin{array}{r} 5\cancel{7}2 \\ -145 \\ \hline 427 \end{array}$$

Approach #2

$$\begin{array}{r} 572 \\ -145 \\ \hline 427 \end{array}$$

Both of these approaches work and have been taught in schools. You probably have learned one of the two.

EXERCISE

Work the following three problems using the approach you have not learned.

$$\begin{array}{r} 392 \\ -174 \end{array} \qquad \begin{array}{r} 831 \\ -264 \end{array} \qquad \begin{array}{r} 94716852 \\ -76386973 \end{array}$$

You might have reacted similarly to the way you reacted to the hand-clasp and arm-folding exercises. Namely,

1. Reluctance — Why should I?
2. Impatience and criticism — This is a stupid way to do this.
3. Completion of the task.
4. Initial awkwardness, but realization that you could not only do it this way once, but also could learn to do it this way if necessary with less awkwardness as you practiced. (The answers are 218, 567, 18329879 — no tricks this time.)

How about a higher-level intellectual problem, one with no single right answer and a higher degree of choice (but still a minor problem)?

E X E R C I S E

Before you turn the page, determine how you would complete the following sequence:

$$\frac{A \quad\quad EF}{BCD \quad G}$$

In other words, how would you place the remaining letters of the alphabet above and below the line to make some kind of sense to you?

Unless you were suspicious that you were being tricked or that there was a "correct" answer, you probably reached a conclusion in a relatively short time. If you think about it, the task you performed was quite impressive. You needed to have knowledge (of alphabets and words), strategies (of patterns and general problem solving), and the ability to make some decisions. Yet you may have reached an answer in a few seconds. The mind is wonderful at handling uncertainty, forming patterns, and reaching decisions. You also probably arrived at a solution that satisfied you and then turned your attention away from the problem and back toward the text. This particular behavior is unconscious (Did you really brood about the suitability of your answer?) and has been called *satisficing*. It is characteristic of human behavior. The mind generally does not compulsively continue to unearth additional options. It sacrifices concepts in order to reach a speedy decision.

In one of his early works, Herbert Simon characterized a satisficer as one who stopped looking through a haystack when he found a needle. An optimizer, on the other hand, would take the whole haystack apart looking for all possible needles in order to be able to pick the sharpest one. Obviously life does not allow us time to completely disassemble all of the haystacks we encounter. However, and this is pertinent to problem solving, our natural behavior may often lead us to the less than sharpest needle.

I have used the ABC problem often with many individuals and groups. They reach an answer in a short time and then satisfice. Some of their answers are summarized here:

A. *Group size*

    1. <u>A   EF   HIJ   </u>   <u>1 2 3 </u>   etc.
       BCD   G   KL   3 1 2

    2. <u>A   EF   KLM</u>   <u>1 2 3</u>   etc.
       BCD   GHIJ   3 4

    3. Random, all on top, all on bottom, or otherwise get it over with.

B. *Letter shapes*

    1. Letters with curved lines below; letters without curved lines above.

    2. Letters with crossbars above; letters without crossbars below.

    3. Letters below can be formed without lifting pencil from paper; letters above cannot.

C. *Sound*

    1. Top letters are soft; bottom letters are hard.

    2. Top letters would take the article *an*; bottom letters would take *a*.

    3. Top letters begin with vowel sound.

D. *Miscellaneous*

    1. <u>A   EF   IJK   </u>   (Top groups begin with vowels.)
       BCD   GH

    2. Move BCDG up and put all on top (or move AEF down and put all on bottom).

    3. People have sung it to me (letters correspond to musical notes).

    4. Bottom letters seem warmer (more friendly).

    5. Top letters are easier to type.

    6. Top letters are initials of western industrialized countries (America, England, France); bottom letters are initials of non-industrialized countries.

    7. Top letters are all in "elephant" (wrong, but wonderful).

What are your reactions to these? Are any of them amusing? Annoying? Wrong? Can you guess why you react the way you do? The answer probably has to do with the fact that you did not think of them. If you satisficed, are you now less satisfied? It is often the case that we become less satisfied with our original answer if the problem seems to be turning into a contest. Satisficing seems to depend somewhat on the rules of the game, and a little conscious thinking can change these rules.

Finally, how did you arrive at the answer(s) you chose. Think about it a while. How much of the process was conscious? You probably remember some conscious thinking that occurred. How much was not conscious? You probably did not consciously pick the problem solving-strategy you used. Did the answer(s) merely "occur" to you? Your mind relied upon its familiar mix of conscious and unconscious activity. It acted habitually.

By now, you are hopefully convinced that problem solving is influenced by habit — that you are programmed to a considerable degree in your thinking. Some of us are more habitual than others. Some of us approach most of our problems with language — wanting to talk them out. Some of us approach our problems quantitatively — hoping for a best answer. However, we are all programmed in our thinking to a remarkable degree by genetics and by our life experience. It should not require too much convincing to get you to agree that groups of people also show symptoms of habitual thinking, as do large organizations. In fact, large organizations typically expend considerable resources in developing problem-solving habits.

If we are optimists, we suspect that habit must be beneficial in life. Not only is it beneficial, but also absolutely necessary to life as we know it. If we consider physical habits, our conscious abilities are simply not rapid enough to control our bodies as we play tennis, a piano concerto, or even walk, eat, or tie our shoes. It is fortunate for us that our brain has a subsystem called the cerebellum, which learns complex combinations of movements and plays them back when needed. These habits, most of which do not require much from our consciousness, allow us to live our complex physical lives.

Similarly, habits allow us to solve intellectual problems much more rapidly than we could if we had to rely completely upon consciousness. We look at 12×12 and 144 appears. We scan printed material and hear it being spoken. We look at a balance sheet and have a sense of the health of the company. We appraise a structure and know that it is a good design. We take one look at a patient and know she is not well. These things we do because we have constructions of knowledge and mental process that are available for our use when we need them. These constructions also minimize our intellectual risk since the ones we have are usually ones that have been tested and found to be successful in the past. In addition, they give us precision as we perform repetitive tasks. Habit, therefore, allows us to move rapidly, accurately, and safely. It would be impossible for us to complete our mental tasks without habit.

Habit also gives us stability. You would not think much of me if you met me each day and each time you met me I was using a totally different set of problem-solving habits. I would be unpredictable and possibly would be considered "insane." In a sense, a schizophrenic is one who discomforts us by constantly changing problem-solving habits. Neither could groups and large organizations acquire their character and uniqueness without habits. Companies worry about their "company culture," which depends on habits. Useful characteristics such as technical sophistication, marketing aggressiveness, and ability to weather economic downturns require habits. Finally, as we will see later, cognitive psychologists are not above counting bits and worrying about how we process information. This worry is a legitimate one because, in a sense, we have a 4-watt mind in a 100-watt world. We cannot process all of the data available to us in raw form. The mind, therefore, depends heavily on structures, models, and stereotypes. These are part and parcel of habit; without habit, we probably couldn't process the information we need in order to exist.

However, the news is not all good. In some situations habits do not serve us well. They certainly stand in opposition to change. By its very nature, change, whether initiated from within ("I have made it in my field and I am ready to move on.") or from without ("The Japanese are increasing their emphasis on personal computer production."), requires a reorientation of habit. Habits are also not always consistent with creativity. Creativity implies deviance from past procedure and therefore is at odds with habit. Also, as will be discussed later, habits can cloud our decision-making capability, decrease our ability to communicate successfully (especially if the communication involves sophisticated expertise), and get in the way of education. Since this is a book on the management of creativity and change, problem-solving habits are central to our discussion.

MODIFICATION OF HABIT

In situations involving change and creativity, we are interested in deviating from habits. In a sense, we want to change our tennis swing. As we have implied, we can do this by using conscious thinking. In the case of a tennis swing, the process is well known. You first come to realize that your swing is not all you might wish. Either your opponents are destroying you, or after studious viewing of television you find that John McEnroe has a more effective serve than yours, or someone you respect comments on the deplorable state of your backhand. Usually the first step in modifying habits is an indication that present habits are not adequate.

The next part of habit modification involves conscious and usually analytical activity. You take lessons, read books, watch videotapes and other tennis players, and learn as much as you can about the "form" you would like as well as the one you presently possess. You then consciously build your new habit. Although it may feel extraordinarily awkward at first, it will presumably take you where you want to go. Finally, you practice your new habit until it becomes a natural and programmed act in its own right. This, of course, does not guarantee a lifetime of satisfaction and winning tennis games. It only means that you are set until the process begins again.

Naturally, such things as reward, punishment, and other types of motivational considerations are important in the process of habit modification. Also involved are time, energy, and perhaps money. However, for the purpose of this discussion, the main thing to note is the centrality of the conscious in modifying habits. Not only is it effective, it is the *only* thing we have to modify habits.

HABIT AND SPECIALIZATION

Both individuals and groups display habits. Becoming aware of problem-solving habits can be a giant step in improving creativity. Happily, we resent being habitual in our approach to problems. We do not like to discover that we are habitual but once we do, we can more easily deal with the unusual. Referring back to Figure 2-1, a knowledge of our habits gains us the upper right-hand corner (knowing we don't know), which is the stepping-off point for creativity. Let us try a problem-solving exercise that will allow you to confront your habits at a higher intellectual plane than the previous exercises in this chapter. You may find yourself resisting it at first, since we tend to dislike operating outside of our usual habits. However, the exercise is an important one and will show you something of the ability to deal with problem-solving habits.

This exercise subjects you to three types of problem solving: verbal-expressive, visual-design, and mathematical. As in past exercises, try to remain aware of how you respond to the three parts of the exercise both cognitively (thinking) and emotionally.

Find a few friends to do this with. It will make the differences in specialization more apparent. The exercise takes about twenty minutes. If you have a representative group of friends, everyone will feel somewhat uncomfortable during at least one of the five-minute exercises. Some of you may not like any of them. All three of the activities you will do require creativity, are of high status, and earn people fame and money. However, to the extent that you feel uncomfortable doing one of them, you probably avoid such activities and do not communicate too well with those who enjoy them. We tend to stay within our habits, with an accompanying loss of creativity.

EXERCISE

1. Spend five minutes writing a short and serious poem on love. Strive for beauty and expression. At the end of five minutes, read your poems to each other.
2. Spend five minutes designing (graphically — draw it on paper) a better desk lamp. Desk lamps usually have shortcomings, whether functional or aesthetic. Draw one that is both functionally successful and beautiful. At the end of the time, show your design to the others in the group and discuss it for a few minutes.
3. Spend five minutes working on the following problem: An ant is in a top corner of a square room that measures 24 ft on a side and is 8 ft high. He sees an edible crumb at the opposite bottom corner. The ant wants to walk to the crumb over the shortest possible path. How long is the path? After the five minutes are over, make sure that everyone in the group understands and agrees upon the answer.

Our reaction to intellectual problems does not necessarily reflect our present ability to solve them. We have all manner of outdated measures and anxieties that influence us. I often give the poetry portion of the exercise to engineering and business students, professional engineers and managers, and business executives. The initial response of the group to the assignment typically runs the gamut from horror to an urgent need to leave the room. However, as the participants begin working on their poems, they find that the process is less painful than they might have thought. They have long-dormant habits remaining from previous schooling with which to construct poetic forms. They also find that they have a lot to say about love, although it may not be information that is consistent with their usual communication habits. The pain returns, however, when they have to divulge their poems to others. After they have read their poems to each other, I usually find that if I ask those whose poems were terrible to raise their hands, all hands are raised. If I then ask the same of those who heard a poem that was surprisingly good, all hands will again be raised. In other words, they all think their own poems are terrible but that those written by the other people are pretty good.

I am coordinator of the Stanford Engineering Executive Program, which is oriented toward managers in technology-based companies. One of the faculty members in the program is Diane Middlebrook, who is a professor of English at Stanford. She introduces the participants to poetry in a minicourse consisting of readings, outside writing, and about four hours of lecture. This is the advanced version of the exercise described previously. Diane often begins by reading the group a poem, and even the process of listening to poetry being read causes them discomfort. Needless to say, their initial attempts at writing are painful. However, the beauty is there. Through a process of pleading, cajoling, explaining, praising, and criticizing, as well as the application of understanding and humor, Diane coaxes the reluctant group to write increasingly sophisticated verse. Figure 4-1 contains short examples written by participants of the 1985 program. A few amateur poets and a great change in everyone's viewpoint toward their own poetry habits usually result from the experience of taking the minicourse.

Many people who feel terribly inadequate writing poetry are capable of constructing acceptable verse. They are merely suffering from lack of confidence in their own ability and the remnants of the social climate that inhibited poetry in high school. Similarly, awkwardness with drawing may result from a confusion between the type of drawing that most people do and the drawing of professional artists; awkwardness with math may result from that long-ago day when a relative lack of speed in calculation (which does not have that much to do with mathematics) caused one to slide from one's rightful spot at the head of the third grade class.

I am sometimes amused at the creativity and energy people will expend in order to avoid a particular style of problem solving with which they do not feel comfortable. A student submitted the short poem on love shown in Figure 4-2. Clever, but probably more taxing than writing the poem.

Another student submitted a paper in response to the desk lamp assignment. It began, "Before you can appreciate my desk-lamp design, it is essential that you understand a few concepts from circuit design, solid state theory, and optics" (obviously a high-tech desk lamp). This was followed by five pages of information from circuit design, solid state theory, and optical theory. However, there was no lamp design. After spending the alloted time telling me what he

FIGURE 4-1 Poems by Students in the Stanford Engineering Executive Program, 1985

Shapely brown bicycling legs
Flashing in the sun through Stanford arches
I am an old man

I comb my hairs with a ball point pen
aging ego
hostage to ratted locks

Fern Hill, you stir the little boy
Take me back
Leave me by the stream above the cliffs
Let me relive the year
The joy; my friends; my dog
. . . no chores!

economic elements of engineering arouse
    me, Anne
eleemosynary music modifies my
    arousal, Anne
elegant eulogies/expert algorithms/
    integrated implantation
    Anne, Anne, Anne

Cherub face glowing to the world,
inner thoughts not expressed.
A filling sponge, thirsty.

Cold night falls on deep snow
Narrow path lit by fuil moon
Dog barks into silence

Paint the sky
Roll the meadow
Fathom the depths
Water under the bridge
No U turn!

Personal perks, privileges.
Mission seduced integrity.
Beguiled by a lofty
Self-esteem through arrogance
Clouded vision. Exquisite
Rationalization. A
Talent squandered, a life disrupted.
Power corrupts.

Invent bad verse—why?
To manifest our joy
before this episode ends.

FIGURE 4-2 A Short Poem on Love

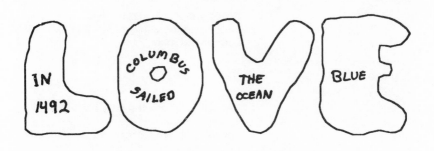

knew, the student conveniently avoided the process of visual imagery.

I clearly remember the response of an alumnus of Stanford to a math puzzle involving two trains. The puzzle hypothesized two trains one mile apart on a single straight track, each traveling at ten miles per hour toward the other. A fly, which had been riding on the front of one, takes off and flies toward the other at twenty miles per hour. Upon reaching the other (which is now less than one mile from the first train), the fly instantly turns and flies back to its original train, at which point it instantly turns again, etc., etc., etc. The puzzle asks how far the fly flies before it is crushed in the train collision. This puzzle obviously has to do with mathematics. Like the one in the exercise, however, it requires insight. The one in the exercise is best approached by imagining that the room is folded out flat as shown in Figure 4-3. If you remember the Pythagorean theorem for a triangle, the answer can be seen to be forty feet. This requires memory. However, the problem with the fly and the train is straightforward. It is merely necessary to realize that each train will travel one-half mile before they collide. Since the trains are traveling ten miles per hour, this will require 1/20th of an hour. The fly is traveling twenty miles per hour. In 1/20th of an hour the fly will fly one mile. However, the answer from the alumnus was:

> Free capricious soaring fly,
> why oh why
> did you have to die?

Once again, a rather wonderful answer to the problem. In fact, just the type of thing I would like to see people do in classes and workshops emphasizing creativity. However, I suspect that the motivation

FIGURE 4-3 The Shortest Possible Path to the Crumb

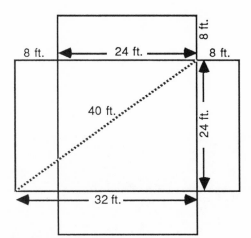

here was not so much creativity as a desire to not spend the time thinking mathematically.

The bottom line of this exercise should be clear. It is a demonstration of the message of this chapter. Our habits, which are not necessarily directly correlated to our abilities, inhibit us from traveling in new directions. They can be consciously overcome, with the result that we can engage in more creative activities. The bad news is that overcoming them requires first of all overcoming emotional signals and, secondly, becoming more of a novice than we are used to being. In Chapter 6, we will discuss habits as a potential resource in problem solving. Habits, after all, have something to do with specialties, and new combinations of specialties can result in new solutions. However, the message of this chapter is that in seeking to increase creativity one should be suspicious of habit; an awareness of the nature of habit and its management is a powerful weapon for the person seeking to increase creativity.

The next chapter will be concerned with memory. Information is necessary for solving problems. Unfortunately, not only is our information restricted by the nature of the senses and processed somewhat automatically by the brain, but it is also arranged in a traditional and structured way in the memory. Since creativity requires new combinations of information, we must be concerned with the nature of memory and techniques to obtain information in fresh combinations.

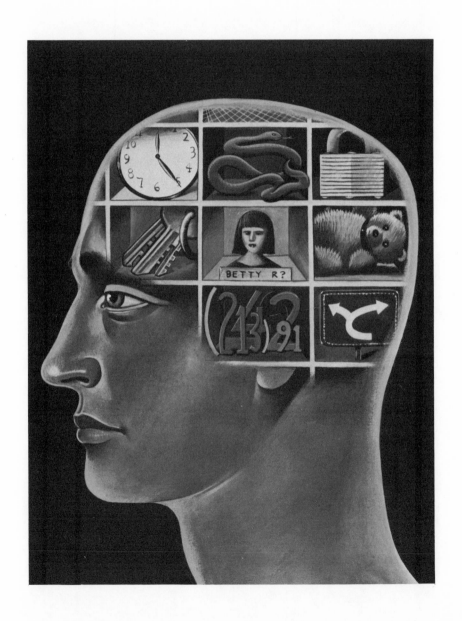

5

Memory — Boxes of Information

THE NATURE OF MEMORY

It should be no surprise that we arrange information outside of our memories to be consistent with the arrangement inside. Our best concept of a memory system seems to be a hierarchical system that files information according to degree of association — the Dewey decimal approach to life. The Dewey decimal system is excellent for traditional disciplines — find one psychology book and the shelf is filled with others. However, it is not as good for nontraditional topics like creativity.

The exact mechanisms of memory are presently a subject of hot debate. Familiarity with the electronic computer causes many people to suppose that memory operates electrically. This argument is strengthened by the measurable electrical activity of the mind and the electrochemical nature of the neuron. However, the random access memory in the computer is much more transient than many of our memories, since it disappears if somebody pulls the plug. As previously mentioned, the biological community thinks that much of memory is in the form of chemical modification along particular neuron pathways. It is possible, as will be discussed later, that both mechanisms are operational and important. However, we do not know the answer. We also do not know the location of memory in the brain, the type of coding used to store sensory experience in the brain, or the method of storage and retrieval by which the brain organizes, files, finds, and presents information to our conscious.

However, experiments have shown us some of the overall characteristics of memory and, from these experiments, we can conclude quite a bit about the effects of memory on problem solving. Let us first talk about three types or stages of memory that have been isolated experimentally and that appear repeatedly in the literature. These three types interrelate closely and may, in fact, be different operations performed by the same machine, but we will discuss them separately.

Sensory Registers

Figure 5-1 shows a diagram of memory as it might be drawn by a cognitive psychologist. The first stage of memory takes place in the sensory registers. Information recorded by the senses is held reasonably intact for a short period of time (a fraction of a second) until it can be sorted and further processed. The information held in the register is unprocessed. A typical psychological experiment demonstrating this presented experimental subjects with a brief (50 millisecond) glimpse of an array of nine letters such as the one shown here:

$$
\begin{array}{ccc}
B & M & R \\
J & S & P \\
F & X & L
\end{array}
$$

Immediately after the array was presented, the subjects were asked to recall the letters and, on the average, could name about half of them. However, if the subjects were asked to recall only one row of the array (designated *immediately after* the exposure to the array by a sound signal), they could recall almost one hundred percent of the row. This meant to the experimenter that the entire array faded from the sensory register too fast for the subjects to recall all of the letters, but not so fast that they couldn't recall any one of the rows completely. Plots of this data show that the partial report allows more recall than the complete report, but the difference decays rapidly over time. The vivid image of unprocessed visual information that

FIGURE 5-1 The Human Memory System

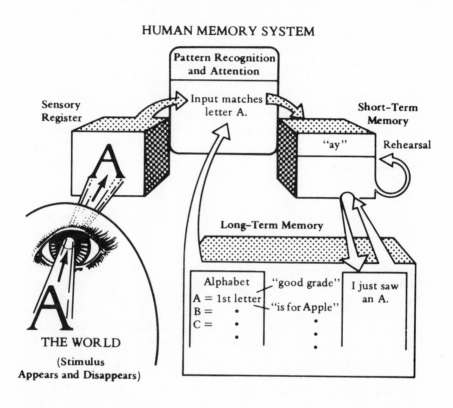

HUMAN MEMORY SYSTEM

lives in memory for a fraction of a second is often referred to as the *icon*. Corresponding auditory information, which has also been demonstrated experimentally, is referred to as the *echo*. Presumably the other senses behave in a similar manner.

The existence of registers and briefly existing images allows the brain the necessary time to make decisions as to which information is important and to transfer that information to its destination. What is the nature of the process that causes us to use certain information from our registers and allows the rest to decay and disappear forever? It cannot be random. It seems far more reasonable to believe that the process is guided by information already in memory.

Short-Term Memory or STM*

Short-term memory is a process that allows us to remember a relatively small amount of information for a few seconds. The time capacity of STM is much longer than that of the registers, but its information capacity is much less. The integer-remembering exercise in the last chapter was a good example.

As we found in this exercise, coding helps short-term memory capacity a great deal. We use this technique constantly and automatically. Returning to telephone numbers, I believe that one of the reasons for the massive resistance to the change from word prefixes (Riverside 9-1403) to all-number dialing (749-1403) is that the word prefix conveniently coded the first two symbols, thereby making the number easier to remember. Try the following:

E X E R C I S E

Recall your automobile license plate in sets of two. Note the mental effort. That was because you probably had to "rechunk" your plate number so you could recall it and consciously break it into a different sequence. For instance, many states issue plates consisting of a group of three letters and a group of three numbers. If you had such a plate and remembered its number in a form XYZ-123, you would have consciously had to repackage it as XY-Z1-23.

If you repeat the short-term memory exercise in the last chapter (the digits), you will probably notice that even though you are dealing with vision (written characters on a page) you held the information in your short-term memory as sounds. You silently spoke the names of the letters to yourself as you read and recalled them as sounds. We seem to store verbal material in our short-term memory as sounds rather than visual images of the printed words. In short-term memory we tend to confuse letters such as *b* and *v*, which have similar sounds. Finally, you noticed that short-term memory is finite in time. It was

---

*The dual-mode memory model, in which functions are separated into short-term and long-term memory is by no means universally accepted. For instance, another school of thought considers memory in the context of depth of processing. In this theory, an item entering memory is analyzed in various stages. The early stages analyze the perceptual characteristics of the information, and later stages analyze its meaning and its fit with information already in memory. The deeper the analysis, the more likely the retention in memory. For the sake of the discussion in this book, we will refer to short-term and long-term memory because the dual-mode model is consistent with observable memory phenomenon.

difficult to recall the sequences of digits after a minute or so had passed.

The mechanism of short-term memory plays a critical role in thinking and problem solving. One experimenter found that when subjects were asked to form an impression of a person on the basis of a single meeting, they tended to describe the person with approximately seven plus or minus two characteristics. The process of retaining material in short-term memory also apparently uses the same equipment used in consciously solving problems. You can gain a sense of this by attempting to remember one number (8627359) while you multiply 63 by 7. In attempting such a task, one finds how easy it is to saturate conscious thinking and short-term memory with competing conscious tasks.

Long-Term Memory

Since our life is greatly affected by the nature of the material in our long-term memory, let us examine how it is selected from our experience for storage. The following exercise will help. You will need a pencil and paper to do it.

EXERCISE

Read the following list of words just once. Do not study them. Simply read each one to yourself in order. Then close the book and write down as many of the words as you recall in whatever order they occur to you.

can, church, house, orange, table, sky, rock, quick, brown, fox, coronary, chin, knob, year, cancer, field, cat, Beethoven, flower, hill, penis, wine, dog, president, car, nose, divorce, apple, sheep, mouse, tree

---

Since there are more than seven words you probably did not remember them all. However, there are several effects that may have determined which ones you did remember. There is a *primacy* and a *recency* effect. You were more likely to remember the word at the beginning of the list and at the end. The explanation for the primacy effect is that you had a clean slate when you began. The reason for the recency effect is that there was less interference between the words at the end of the list and the recall time than between the ones in the middle of the list and the recall time. Figure 5-2 shows these effects at work during a lecture. Students remembered a great deal of the material presented at the first and the end of the period,

FIGURE 5-2 The Primacy and Recency Effects

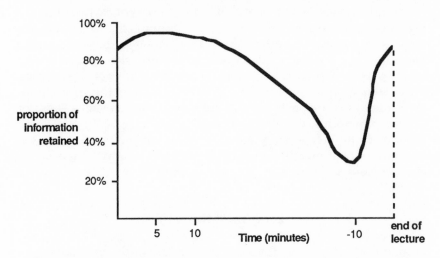

A study by E. J. Thomas showed that after a lecture students best recall material presented at the beginning of it (the primacy effect) or at the end (the recency effect). As a rule, the later the material is presented, the less able students are to recall it.

but their ability to recall dipped drastically in the middle. It should be quite simple for you to apply this phenomenon to a meeting. If you are trying to make a point that people will remember, make it either early or late. If the meeting is to convey important information, make sure you take good notes in the middle. If it is your meeting and you want the people attending to remember a large amount of information, do not bother to run continuously for two or three hours. Breaks have intellectual as well as emotional value.

The primacy and recency effects can be explained by the dual-mode memory model. It is probable that when information is first acquired in memory it is rehearsed in short-term memory (since nothing else is there to interfere with rehearsal) and therefore is more likely to be transferred to long-term memory. In our exercise, at the end of information acquisition the last items might still have been in short-term memory and have been recalled from there. The middle items were not rehearsed because short-term memory was full and the information was not retained in short-term memory because more was entering. This explanation is consistent with experimental findings that if subjects are forced to do some other activity, such as arithmetic, after information is presented, the recency effect will decrease markedly.

You might also have remembered words that stood out from the rest of the list (Beethoven, penis). This is called the Von Restorff effect, after a psychologist who experimented with various types of lists and found that words or numbers were remembered better if surrounded with symbols of a different type. You might have recalled words from the list that were personally important to you — that were accompanied by some sort of emotion when you read them. Finally, you might have remembered quick brown fox, since the three words were presented in a structure with which you are familiar.

These effects should make you suspicious about the information in your memory and your probable use of it. They should also give you some clues as to how to make better use of your memory ca-pability. The primacy and recency effects tell us that we may be fooling ourselves if we try to educate ourselves about a new topic by sitting down and reading a textbook from beginning to end. Even if we figure out the material as we go along and understand the con-cepts, we may remember very little of it, especially that in the middle of the book. There are good reasons why students receive their education in short chunks called classes, and why material is spaced out with reinforcing discussions, problems, and papers. Recency and primacy are a rationale for good things such as recesses, coffee breaks, lunches, and vacations. You might also expect that your memory contains material that you have remembered because it was unique in its context when you encountered it.

Let us now say a few words about the effects of importance on long-term memory. Our mind contains a very complex priority list as to what type of information we remember. We remember first of all things that are directly involved with survival and physical well-being. As an example, consider driving to work in the morning. Ordinarily we remember very little of the drive, since it is rote activity that can be done by learned responses under the control of the unconscious. However, should something occur that threatens our safety, such as a truck coming towards us in our lane, we remember it very clearly indeed. Think about your first childhood memory. It is probably vivid. It probably also is a traumatic event, possibly accompanied by some threat to safety. We tend to also remember things involved with the survival of others. We tend to remember events accompanied with high emotional level of any sort — events accompanied by great joy, sadness, conflict, frustration, or fear.

Beyond that, we have personal priority systems tailored to our sense of the relative importance of certain types of information to our success in life. This priority system can be changed to fit our needs and often is. For instance, when you decide to buy a new car, motorcycle, sewing machine, or dishwasher it is relatively easy to

remember material concerning the product that previously would
have been difficult to remember, had you even noticed it. The initial
prerequisite for memory is attention, and attention follows motivation. We may change our priority system because we are bored,
because we want something more in life, because we received a new
assignment on the job, because we move, have children, go through
a divorce, or have a friend die. However, whatever it is at a certain
time, this priority system is a powerful determinant on the information we remember. Someone with severe math anxiety may read
one of the well-written simplified math books now available, but may
remember very little. Mathematics is simply at the bottom of their
priority list. It might be nice to know a tremendous amount about
art, but we are not about to go through the effort involved unless it
is truly important to us, because we will spend weeks and months
reading material that we will remember very poorly, if at all. How
much do you remember from classes in high school that you considered unimportant to you? Contrast your recall with that from classes
you considered important at the time.

Now a few words about structure. It is here that we gain great
insight into the problem-solving process. As we mentioned in the
short-term memory discussion, structure allows us to code and,
therefore, put more material into our short-term memories. Structure
is similarly powerful in transferring information to long-term memory. We use many structural schemes, but they all serve the same
purpose. They allow us to organize disparate information into for-
mats that are consistent with the mechanism of our memory. The
following exercise shows how increasingly easy a meaningless list
becomes as it is first parsed (made consistent with grammatical structure already in the mind) and then finally given meaning (consistently with experience in our memory).

EXERCISE

Remember the following list. Read it and close the book. Then see if you can
repeat it to yourself.

saw, when, panicked, Jim, ripped, haystack, the, relaxed, when, cloth, the,
but, he

I assume that this was not only difficult, but also that your brain
resisted such an apparently useless exercise. However, I will now
make these words into a relatively meaningless sentence and, al-

though the sentence may seem both dumb and amusing, you will be able to remember it more easily.

Remember the following sentence. Read it and close the book. Then see if you can repeat it to yourself.

Jim panicked when the cloth ripped, but relaxed when he saw the haystack.

However, your brain, although more cooperative, still is not completely satisfied. It seeks meaning or consistence with some logical structure already within memory. I can give your brain this meaning through a simple phrase — parachute jumping. You have a structure for parachute jumping that will make the sentence meaningful, and when you now return and read it again, you will be happy. Also you will be more easily able to remember the sentence over a long period. See if you can recall it when you awaken tomorrow morning.

Structure explains the seemingly incredible mental abilities of experts. Champion chess players, for instance, can remember the positions of the pieces on the board during a game after a brief glance. Amateurs cannot. However, the ability of the chess masters is built on their experience with the game. They recall the chess pieces in structural segments that are associated with tactical situations. They are no better than the amateurs at recalling the position of chess pieces placed on the board in random configurations.

It is also possible to manufacture and learn structures to aid in memorizing disparate facts. Mnemonics are an example of this. These are jingles or statements that provide a rememberable structure upon which we can hang otherwise meaningless quantities. Examples are the mnemonics used by medical students to remember anatomy. There is even a pocket-sized book of them. It tells you, for instance, that if you remember "Please, Can Soft Soap Remove Tint In Ladies' Stockings," you have given structure to the branches of the abdominal aorta (Phrenics, Coeliac artery, middle Suprarenal, Superior mesenteric, Renal, Testicular, Inferior mesenteric, Lumbar, middle Sacral).

Most memory improvement techniques utilize structures. One of the older ones is the method of loci. In this technique, a number of locations is learned through visiting each and carefully inspecting the local environment. Typically, we take a walk through familiar surroundings, choosing 15 to 20 points as loci. After returning from the walk, it should be possible to clearly remember and visualize each location, since the structure of the walk and of familiar surroundings allows this degree of memory without too much effort. Then, in order to remember a list of disparate items, it is only necessary to visualize each of them in one of the loci. As you mentally retake the walk, the objects should become clear. This technique was described by Quintillian in about 50 A.D. He wrote, "The first notion is placed, as it were, in the forecourt; the second, let us say, in the atrium; the remainder . . . committed not only to bedrooms and parlours, but even to statues and the like. This done, when it is required to revive the memory, one begins from the first place to run through all, demanding what has been entrusted to them, of which one will be reminded by the image."

Books on memory improvement typically ask you to learn similar structures so that you can then associate unfamiliar items with them. These techniques are all effective. However, they are seldom used because most of us prefer to rely on the structures we already possess, rather than learn new ones.

This need for memory structure affects problem solving in two ways. First, we are likely to remember information that is consistent with data already in our memories. If we have no hook on which to hang new information, it is difficult to deal with. This need for consistency, coupled with our previously discussed priorities, will cause us to continue to specialize in our present directions. If we are an oenophile, we have more structure to collect information on wine than if we are not. The oenophiles will, therefore, tend to become more sophisticated while the rest of us will have more and more difficulty dealing with them on the subject of wine. If an individual knows no math, it is less likely that math information will be retained.

Second, structure is involved in the system by which information is retrieved from memory. Information seems to be stored with other information ordinarily associated with it. What comes to your mind when I give you the word *waiter*. Think a bit. Are items usually associated with restaurants coming to mind? Did you think of menu, tablecloths, silver, candles, tips, wine, food, and bills? Did you by chance think of a runover dead cat, a furnace, or a farm tractor? Probably not only did you not think of such things, but they seem incongruous in the "waiter" context. That is because these objects are not in the file in your memory that contains waiter. Had I mentioned menu, tips, or fine food, you might have still reached the concept of waiter. The words are related and therefore easily accessible. However, you would still have had trouble with dead cats, furnaces, and farm tractors.

This filing system, which is hierarchical in nature, is not only efficient in its ordinary transfer of information, but also is the only type of system we are able to conceptualize for the storage and retrieval of large amounts of information. However, it makes it difficult for disparate concepts to come together. This inhibits creativity. Try the following problem-solving exercise. Initially, your mind will resist the requested thinking activity with all kinds of negative feelings and elaborate rationales. However, as you persevere, you will find that you can think in the required way, but that it is difficult. The next thing you may notice is that the ideas you produce are somewhat "flaky," that they may seem impractical, silly, or embarrassing. However, you may also notice some ideas that appear fairly original and lead to concepts that may even seem practical. You will be creative using a technique that breaks mental set by forcing you to cross file boundaries in your memory. This is not the type of activity that occurs naturally. The structure of the normal filing system can inhibit creative problem solving.

E X E R C I S E

Assume that you have been hired as a consultant by a restaurant that is having business problems. See how many ways you can think of to improve the business of the restaurant using the concept of a runover dead cat.

Did you notice the stages? They were probably initial emotional resistance followed by effort and, finally, by "flaky" ideas (placing dead cats on the steps of the competitor's restaurant, naming the restaurant "The Dead Cat" in an exotic language, moving the restaurant closer to a highway, catering to "sickies," or providing cat-sitting services). Do not be deterred by "flakiness." One of the underlying theories of creativity techniques is that wild ideas are valuable because the normal forces of life will tend to convert them rapidly into practicality.

A word that is found in discussions of structure in problem solving is "stereotyping." We tend to make heavy use of stereotypes or generalizations in our thinking. This allows us to think at a more abstract level and handle detailed information more easily. We may neglect, forget, or rationalize away information that does not fit our stereotypes. Information that does fit can be conveniently hung on a framework. Without stereotypes we probably could not handle the amount of information in our lives. However, the bad news is that stereotyping hampers us in acquiring specific information about individual characteristics that are not consistent with stereotypes. It continues to allow us to harbor erroneous notions about ethnic or racial groups, women, men, motorcycle riders, football players, homosexuals, college professors, psychiatrists, schizophrenics, and monks. Stereotyping inhibits our ability to deal with new material, objects, and situations. However, these stereotypes are very powerful in the mechanics of our memories.

Stereotypes are related to our tendency to complete, or add to and modify information that we receive in order to have consistent models. We are capable of inferring things based on our total store of memory. We are used to adding details to inputs in order to better understand them. In other words, we may add meaning to incoming items in order to better store them. If someone tells us that he or she saw a drunk staggering along main street with a bottle, we assume that it was a liquor, wine, or beer bottle and not a baby bottle. We seek consistency so that our stereotypes will be effective. For instance, a psychology experiment was conducted in which subjects were shown a film of a traffic accident and then later asked questions about it. Some of them were asked, "How fast were the cars going when they hit each other?" The others were asked, "How fast were the cars going when they smashed into each other?" Needless to say, the latter group recalled much more destruction than the former. We often infer data that is missing or ignore data that is present in order to be consistent with our stereotypes.

The Nature of Forgetting

How about forgetting? We have talked about remembering, but obviously the process of forgetting also shapes the information and techniques available to us to solve our problems. The mechanisms of forgetting are even less well understood than the mechanisms of remembering. One of the older theories is that of decay — that over time the process that causes memory slowly degrades. The reactions, if chemical, slowly reverse. The materials, if protein, slowly erode. The signals, if electric, slowly decrease in magnitude. This theory has its problems, because information is not uniformly erased by time. We can easily recall our first childhood memory, but we probably cannot remember what we were doing the next day or maybe even the next year.

Newer theories rely more on interference and changing retrieval cues. New information complicates or interferes with the process of retrieval, or the passage of time alters the cues that we use to retrieve information. The interference theory can easily be demonstrated in the laboratory. Experiments have been done in which two groups of people learned lists of nonsense words. After a given time had passed, they were tested on their recall. However, one of the groups had learned a second list in the interim. This second group showed a much lower ability to recall. According to interference theory, the absent-minded professor is merely suffering from an overload of information (my explanation, incidentally, because professors are bombarded with constant input from hundreds of people; future, present, and past classes; administrative tasks; and our own projects).

According to the people who explain forgetting by changes in retrieval cues, the passage of time alters the cues that cause us to retrieve our information. This might explain why memories come flooding back if we visit our old elementary school or meet old friends we have not seen in years. It is quite believable that our situations in life change so that we no longer have the same reference point from which to access details in our memory. It seems to me that the explanation might involve both these mechanisms plus some sort of decay. Neither the interference nor the retrieval cue theories satisfactorily explain why experts such as chess players become "rusty" over time.

Finally we should not leave this topic without briefly discussing recognition. It is possible to recognize people, situations, and objects even though they cannot be recalled. Of the large number of people you have met in your life, you probably can recall only a small fraction. Yet it is not unusual to encounter people and "recognize" them from a long-ago encounter. An amazing set of psychology experiments showing the power of recognition involved showing experimental subjects over five hundred words, each printed on a card. The subjects looked through the cards in order. They were then given a series of sixty-two alternative tests, which tested recognition of the words. The mean accuracy rate was 88 percent. Another experiment utilized 612 colored pictures and resulted in a recognition accuracy of 97 percent. These figures are very high compared with recall figures. However, recognition can be influenced by the structuring and stereotyping mentioned earlier. In one of his books, I. M. L. Hunter provided a familiar account of the effect of stereotyping on recall. "In the week beginning 23 October, I encountered in . . . the University a male student of very conspicuous Scandinavian appearance. . . . I recall being very forcibly impressed by [his] nordic, Viking-like appearance — his fair hair, his blue eyes, his long bones. . . . On several occasions . . . I recalled his appearance in connection with a Scandinavian correspondence I was then conducting and thought of him as the 'perfect Viking,' visualizing him at the helm of a long-ship crossing the North Sea in quest of adventure. [When I again saw the man on 23 November,] I did not recognize him and he had to introduce himself. It was not that I had forgotten what he looked like but that his appearance, as I recalled it, had become grossly distorted. . . . [H]e was very different from my recollection of him. His hair was darker, his eyes less blue, his build less muscular, and he was wearing spectacles (as he always does)."

MANAGEMENT OF MEMORY IN PROBLEM SOLVING

Memory is presently the subject of intense study, and the conclusions that are emerging confirm our suspicions that we are heavily programmed in our problem solving. Our memories contain the information necessary for creativity and response to change. However, traditional priorities, structures, and access programs are not always likely to give us the desired combinations. We once again should suspect that conscious effort is necessary to overcome the business-as-usual nature of the mechanisms of memory and that knowledge of memory is necessary in order to be effective in this effort.

The creative problem solver should keep the following in mind:

1. Memory attempts to make life easier by arranging information according to usual associations. Material recalled from memory in an automatic mode is, therefore, unlikely to be arranged in creative combinations.
2. Memory contains more information than one is aware of.
3. New combinations can be consciously made, either by manipulating raw information recalled from memory or by using set-breakers such as those described in Chapter 7.

This chapter is consistent with the last three in describing behavior in terms that make us seem habitual and programmed. The last portion of the book has to do with modifying or circumventing these habits. However, the habits themselves can often be used to better advantage in creative problem solving. The next chapter discusses this issue.

PART TWO

DOING

1560

6

Specialization as a
Problem-Solving Resource

Remember the exercise in Chapter 4 that asked you to try three different styles of thinking? There are, of course, many more than three. Table 6-1 lists adjectives that might be applied to the word *thinking*. These words also imply problem-solving styles or thinking specialities. The list is by no means complete; it is included to give you an indication of some types of specialties. The first column contains words that describe thinking strategies and methods of attacking problems. The second column consists of words that are often used to describe thinking but which are obviously reflections on personality. Upon compiling this list, I was astounded by the number of words that have negative personality connotations. See if you can add some with positive connotations. The third column refers to disciplinary specializations. These are often related to the schooling we have had and the way we make our living. This column has the potential to be extremely long, of course, because we have all developed specializations that help us be proficient in our jobs. The fourth column contains words that refer to the overall quality of thinking. The last is a miscellaneous column.

As you read the words, notice which ones cause you positive or negative emotion. The positive ones are probably consistent with

TABLE 6-1 Thinking

Strategic	Personality Related	Disciplinary	Overall Quality	Miscellaneous
Inductive	Optimistic	Scientific	Quick	Visual
Deductive	Pessimistic	Humanistic	Slow	Wishful
Critical	Paranoid	Mathematical	Sloppy	Tough-
Intuitive	Neurotic	Verbal	Keen	minded
Analytic	Compulsive	Legal	Fuzzy	Literal
Imaginative	Obsessive	Medical	Clear	Expressive
Converging	Schizophrenic	Technological	Right	Exaggerated
Diverging	Twisted	Anthropological	Shallow	Random
Rational	Warped	Sociological	Deep	Instinctive
Irrational	Distorted	Historical	Methodical	Insightful
Forward	Pigheaded	Market-oriented	Plodding	Constructive
Backward	Wrong-headed	Product-oriented	Brilliant	Aesthetic
Focused	Stubborn	People-oriented	Mercurial	Creative
Narrow	Maudlin	Financial	Muddled	Efficient
Broad	Introverted		Productive	Precise
Incisive	Extroverted		Powerful	Innovative
Decisive	Weird			Practical
Indecisive	Sick			
Judgmental	Kinky			
Theoretical	Aggressive			
Applied				
Additive				
Eliminative				
Qualitative				
Quantitative				
Objective				
Subjective				

your preferred problem-solving habits. Which styles are consistent with being able to adapt to change and be creative? Which ones are consistent with the status quo? Which ones do you admire the most? Which ones would you like more of? Can you think of words that should be added to the list? Would you like to see some words deleted? Can you think of a better list format? See if you can list your own preferred and nonpreferred problem-solving specialties and those of your friends and the members of your household.

Intellectual specialization is valuable to us. Specialties are psychologically healthy. If you are extraordinarily good at something, you are likely to have a much healthier ego. A common example of this is the apparently fearless venturing of highly credentialled people (Nobel-prize winners, ex-presidents of large corporations, professional athletes, politicians) into areas for which they have little if any formal training or even competence. Specialties are also socially invaluable. It is simply not possible to maintain the complex social institutions we have without specialization. Organizations would obviously not be able to function as they do without people who have become extremely specialized and, therefore, proficient in their fields. Neither could our nations, our cities, our schools, or even our homes.

THE PROBLEMS OF SPECIALIZATION

What's good for mom or General Motors may not be good for everyone else. Intellectual specialities are sometimes described as "grooves" in the mind caused by repetition and reward. This is an old metaphor probably tracing back to William James and now a part of our vocabulary (the "grooved" swing). Unfortunately, a groove is not too far from a rut. Many of the problems I see are a result of people attempting to inflict their own specialties on others or on the world and/or not appreciating the value of the specialties of others. A professional example can be seen in many companies in the interaction (or lack of) between marketing and new product development. Both of these activities are necessary in a healthy company and, in fact, many companies get into trouble when one function tends to dominate at the wrong time. However, the specializations of the people involved tend to lead them into different philosophies. To product-development people, progress is improvement in the product itself, whether it be functional, visual, or economic. Their focus is internal, toward the company design, development, manufacturing capability, and pertinent technology.

Marketing people, on the other hand, have an outward focus. They are tuned to customer needs, which may not be consistent with technical progress. It is possible in a company to find the engineers attempting to develop a faster, more expensive printer and the marketing people calling for a slower, cheaper printer. Should this situation continue, great pain can result. Similar differences in attitude come from the relative specializations of product design and manufacturing people, managers and workers, hardware and software experts, research and product development people, first-line managers and middle managers, line and staff people, professors and students, teenagers and parents, and husbands and wives.

The modern university, where I happen to draw my pay, is perhaps as extravagant an example of such specialization as can be found, and the resulting good news and bad news is readily apparent. Faculty are hired because of their extraordinary competence in their specialty. They are true to their disciplines and view the university as a place to practice their craft. Although interdisciplinary activity is considered to be valuable, it occurs only with agony. The prime reason is that the specialists prefer to compete and work within their own specialty and tend to view other specialties with a bit of contempt. Such representative bodies as academic senates, which typically contain influential people in a wide range of specialties, are often inhibited by an immense amount of self-interest based on academic specialties. Colleges and secondary and primary schools, are, of course, subject to the same problems. Most curricula are eventually set by a power struggle between academic disciplines and, as the secondary and primary levels are reached, politicians and parents join the fray, because they too are "experts" at education and want to inflict their specialties upon the youth of the world.

Parents also attempt to convey their specialties to their children, often with painful results. I am often frustrated as a university professor to see the amount of pressure that some parents put on their children to "follow in their footsteps" (physician, business executive, engineer) when these footsteps have little congruence with the interests and talents of their children. Parents also attempt to impart obsolete social and domestic expertise. Religious leaders and interest groups of all sorts similarly seek to impart their own routines to people even though the routines may no longer be consistent with society.

Even professionals are not above such behavior. I have spent much of my time as a professional engineer attempting to help engineers from various disciplines (mechanical, electrical, civil, etc.) work together on projects. Their own disciplinary expertise makes them particularly unwilling to become educated about the approaches and values of other disciplines and gives them confidence in their own expertise that sometimes exceeds reasonableness.

Professionals from all areas have their own particular specialty, which they tend to push in problem situations and which they attempt to convey to the apprentice. The previous success of these specialties causes communication and creativity problems and inhibits change. It can be blamed for reluctance in the adoption of computers, in the acceptance of the increased control and socialism inherent in a larger and older society, and in the acceptance of changing social values. "The old specialties worked in a simpler time when we were in control. Let's keep the old specialties and we will remain in control and times will remain simple."

This tendency to cling doggedly to a simple specialty is a tragedy because new combinations of specialties are among the more potent resources for increased creativity and change. I consider people to be "intellectual capital." By that I mean that individuals, groups, or organizations represent an intellectual resource that can be used wisely or stupidly. The proper utilization of such resources for creativity and change is different than the proper utilization for business as usual. The concept of a problem-solving habit is a powerful one for understanding this. We unfortunately do not think of people in terms of these habits. In fact, we interact with people at the most general level possible and do not tend to classify them according to what people in universities sometimes call "cognitive style."

Let's think a bit about how we form our opinions about people. When we first encounter someone, we immediately begin to form impressions. They are based on the appearance and behavior of the person, on the context in which we meet them, and on our own personality, experience, expectations, and desires. We are quite capable of making snap judgments and do. Look at Figure 6-1, for instance. Are you making judgments? These judgments are often

FIGURE 6-1 A Person to be Judged

based on physical features and stereotypes. They are useful to us, in that they quickly let us assume certain things about others. They are obviously somewhat accurate, or we would by now have learned not to make them. However, they are unconscious and nonanalytical. We give more credit for positive characteristics to physically attractive people. We have biases based on skin color, gender, physical handicaps, dress, hair style, and all manner of things.

We tend to notice deviations from the norm more than the norm and the bizarre more than the conventional. We also notice characteristics of strangers according to our own personal scheme of priorities. Some of us notice fingernails, some skin, some eyes, some makeup, and some whether the other person smokes or not. Where behavior is concerned, things become even more complex. If we think that environmental causes predominate, we do not associate people as strongly with their behavior as if we think that they behave in a certain way because of choice. We tend to associate the behavior of people we think are strong more with choice and the behavior of people we think are weaker more with environmental causes. We, of course, also interpret this behavior in light of our own purposes. The male might interpret the female's smile differently if she is helping him buy a dress for his wife than if she is sitting next to him in a singles' bar. The point is that not only do we make incredibly quick impressions of people, these impressions are heavily biased by our minds. In one interesting psychological experiment a comparison was made between single observers describing two different children and two different observers describing the same child. The categories used in both cases were compared. The overlap was greater when one person described two children than when two people described one child. In other words, the observer dominated the process by selecting categories that were helpful to and consistent with him, not the children.

Do you believe this? You should, because it is the way you perceive people. Over time, of course, more information is obtained through various relationships and the impression becomes truer. However, it never becomes totally accurate and is never complete. If you are married, don't you still occasionally refuse to accept characteristics of your spouse because they don't fit your model of what your spouse should be? Normal. Also dangerous.

Suppose we were sitting beside each other on an airplane in the first-class compartment and you were reading this book. Suppose further that I was dressed in typical first-class style, noticed you reading this book, asked you if it were interesting, and then mentioned that I had written it. After a few minutes of conversation, suppose that I, with a touch of embarrassment, told you that I had forgotten to bring any cash with me and that I was going to have to take a taxi to town to be on time for a meeting and asked you to lend me $20. Would you lend it to me? What would you use to make this decision? Would it take you long? It is probable that whatever your answer, you would make your decision quickly and not require too much information about me. You would have formed a perception of me on very little data in a very short time and could extrapolate it to whether or not you should lend me the money.

This happened to me once. My seat partner (who requested the loan) was a most impressive person to look at and talk to, and occupied an important position. Since I travel a great deal and occasionally forget things, I instantly loaned him the money. I did not bother to ask him for identification or even for his home address. I especially did not bother to question his honesty. Incidentally, I never received the money back.

You should be happy to know that I would return your money, unless the turmoil of my life caused me to forget to, as I am sure was the case with my seat partner. (I still have not accepted the possibility that the man made a living taking $20 bills from people like me.) Hopefully the personal impression I make, coupled with the probability that confidence men or women who can afford a first-class ticket would not play for $20, would make the loan a good risk. However, I could have spent a little more conscious effort and learned more about the man. Now let me ask you the $64 question. Return to Figure 6-1. What would you say about the intellectual habits of this person? An unusual question? You might respond by saying that intellectual habits are more difficult to assume from physical appearance than behavioral habits. Whether that is true or not, you might also admit that it is more unusual to think of people in terms of intellectual habit.

USING SPECIALIZATION TO INCREASE CREATIVITY

One of the greatest untapped resources in the management of creativity and change is the ability to integrate specialties in a way that gives us greater problem-solving capability than we obtain from the parts. This is the synthesis of problem-solving styles. Let us imagine that we could plot problem-solving styles of individuals in some way such as that shown in Figure 6-2. There are two extreme ways in which such a group of people could operate. One would be at the overlap, making use of problem-solving specialties that are common

FIGURE 6-2 The Problem-Solving Styles of Five Individuals

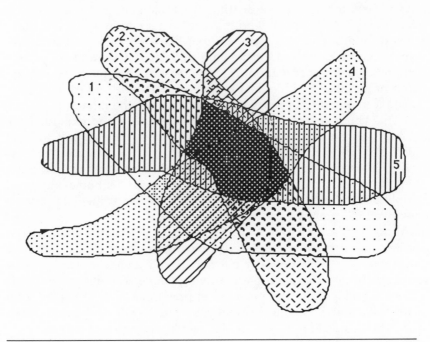

to all members. This is not an uncommon way of operating and in certain situations gives great benefit. An unstructured group of peers will tend to operate in this way. If you have ever played a game called Desert Survival (there are similar ones called Lunar Survival and Arctic Survival), your group probably operated in this way. In this game you are asked to imagine that you are stranded in a hostile place with a group of 15 objects. You are to rank the objects in order of usefulness. You first do it as individuals and then as a group. There are experts in these situations, and the group ranking is usually in closer agreement with the expert rankings than the individual rankings. There are obvious reasons for this. Groups operating in common problem-solving areas are wise, converging, and conservative. They are also smoothly running and quite happy. They are not good at creativity and change because the success of the group is due to its ability to suppress deviance from conventional wisdom.

The other extreme operating mode would be to use the envelope of all of the individual problem-solving styles. In this case, we have an intellectual capability that far surpasses that of any individuals in the group. The group is, if you will, smarter. It is capable of great creativity and change. However, it must be managed carefully because it will obviously be rife with discomfort, disagreement, and divergence. It is, however, a powerful resource and will not be guilty of "group think" if properly managed.

How can such a group come about? By expanding one's acceptable vocabulary of problem-solving styles, an individual can approach such a group. An existing group of people can be brought closer to this mode by encouragement and proper management. However, an even quicker way is through formation of an ad hoc group, a task force, a study team, or other assemblage of people with different intellectual preferences. Such a group begins with the desired variety of cognitive styles. We will discuss this in more detail in Chapter 11, which has to do with organizational and management styles.

Let us talk about problem-solving specialties still more specifically in order to reinforce this message. We will discuss six specific sets of specialties in order to better illustrate what we mean by specialty. These six are typical of broad cognitive style differences that we encounter. There are many others, but if you have an understanding of these, you will be better able to think in terms of cognitive styles and be better equipped to find more productive ways of solving problems in groups.

SCIENTIFIC-HUMANISTIC

Many observers of the intellectual condition divide the population into two parts. Whether this is an indication of people's desire to simplify complex situations or a recognition of the tremendous antagonism between those who exhibit extreme preferences for one mode of thought or the other, I don't know. One of the more well-known divisions is the two-culture concept of C. P. Snow first put forward in his essay "The Two Cultures and the Scientific Revolution." Snow states, "Attempts to divide anything into two ought to be regarded with some suspicion." However, he then sails on to say, "I have thought a long time about going in for further refinements; but in the end I have decided against. I was searching for something a little more than a dashing metaphor, a good deal less than a cultural map; and for those purposes the two cultures is about right."

Snow was a scientist by training and profession who later became a writer. He mixed with literary people and scientists in his life, and these were the poles of his two cultures. In his essay he bemoaned the fact that these two cultures were separate. "Between the two a gulf of mutual incomprehension — sometimes (particularly among the young) hostility and dislike, but most of all lack of understanding." Later he goes on to say, "The non-scientists have a rooted impression that the scientists are shallowly optimistic, unaware of man's condition. On the other hand, the scientists believe that the literary intellectuals are totally lacking in foresight, peculiarly unconcerned with their brother men, in a deep sense anti-intellectual, anxious to restrict both art and thought to the existential moment."

Humanists pledge their faith to the written and spoken word and also place great faith in works that have withstood the test of time. In academia, they disclaim any particular application of their material beyond that of intellectual stimulation and insight into the human condition. To those not within the inner circle, their entire approach to life can be disturbingly smug. As Snow says, "At one pole we have the literary intellectuals, who incidentally while no one was looking took to referring to themselves as 'intellectuals' as though there were no others." They also refer to themselves as those involved in the "humane" disciplines. This gives those in other disciplines the choice between "inhumane," "nonhumane," "unhumane," or other unexciting labels. However, their work is not only important, but central to our society.

On the other hand, practitioners and zealous supporters of science are similarly smug, while pledging their faith to the continuing ability to better understand natural phenomena and to the future. Value is placed on past "great works," but the fate of a scientific document is eventual obsolescence and therefore more value is placed on present works that clarify understanding and break through present limits. Once again, to those not within the inner circle, the practitioners and supporters can appear to verge on the arrogant, with their jargon, techniques, and infuriating confidence.

If we assign other groups to the culture with which they have the most affinity (engineers, for instance, with scientists, historians with the literary, and practitioners of the social sciences divided according to their use of mathematics), we define the modern university. We find words like "fuzzy studies" used to describe the humanities and "softer" social sciences. We find that students use the wonderful word "techy" to describe their colleagues in the natural sciences, engineering, premed, and other programs based on mathematics and the physical sciences. Neither of these words connotes great respect and envy. The subdivision was probably the same when you went to school, although the words differed. Snow's generalities hold true.

Unfortunately, this specialization robs one of the intellectual excitement available to the other camp, and it robs society of the desperately rare and needed person who can balance modern science and humanistic concern. It also robs organizations of the valuable synthesis of the quantitative and the qualitative. An example can be seen in the modern business school. There is much internal jousting between faculty in the "decision sciences" and their more qualitative colleagues. Practicing businessmen align themselves according to their own fondness or lack of same for mathematical approaches. What the world needs is a combination. In particular, what creativity and change need is a combination.

The irony of this particular separation is that it is based at least partly on widespread misunderstanding of the nature of the activities of practitioners of these "two cultures." Much of this is based on the schoolwork that is associated with them. For instance, the type of mathematics and science that one sees through secondary school and usually well into college is rote, single-answer material. Even in calculus, one is asked to learn perfectly mathematics invented by Newton some time ago. This material is certainly important to scientists, engineers, and mathematicians, but only to develop intellectual processes and learn certain techniques. Students get little chance to experience the creative aspects of these fields. They have no idea what is involved in inventing new math (which is what "pure" mathematicians do), designing, developing, and manufacturing new products and services (which is what engineers spend much of their time doing and which is as close to an art as to a science), and making discoveries in science. An entrancing and reasonably honest story of scientific discovery is told in *Double Helix*, a book written by J. Watson about the discovery of the structure of DNA. It chronicles the activities of professional scientists and so flies in the face of common perceptions that it was and remains controversial. Although written by a man who won the Nobel prize for the work described in the book, the Harvard University Press refused to publish it. I use it with students, who are still occasionally offended that Watson did not act like scientists are supposed to act.

Literary people, on the other hand, can be extraordinarily analytical. In particular, those involved in criticism are to a great extent practitioners of a tough-minded, judgmental, information-based discipline. Many writers, visual artists, and musicians are dependent upon abstract and complex theory. Certainly much of musical theory seems close to the popular conception of science. The rules in language are as stringent as the rules in mathematics. Philosophy seems to overlap mathematics. The message is that there is much that is shared in the intellectual processes involved in the work of those involved in Snow's two cultures. The scientists make much use of the right brain and the literary leaders use the left. The scientist is capable of great expression, intuition, and creative insight, and shares the existential problems of the nonscientist. The humanist is capable of analysis, technique, and tight, unyielding criteria.

ANALYSIS-SYNTHESIS

Strictly speaking, the word *analysis* refers to the separation of the whole into its parts so as to discover the characteristics of these parts and their relationship to each other and to the whole. In this way, it is possible to develop an understanding of the behavior of the whole as a function of its parts. A clear demonstration of this can be seen in mathematics such as calculus where variables (the parts) are specifically defined and then worked with through equations to find the relationships between them. Analysis is widely used in science, literature, and all other fields. It is high-level human intellectual activity, and phrases such as "let's analyze this" and "analytical thinking" are everywhere.

Synthesis refers to the putting together of parts into a whole. The purpose of synthesis is to come up with a construct to satisfy the goal. An example of pure synthesis, if it exists, would be a painting by a child or the axe of very primitive man. I say "if it exists" because ordinarily even the most basic acts of synthesis are accompanied by some knowledge or rules based on analysis. The child has probably been shown that he or she should not move the brush toward the bristle end, and the primitive person probably analyzed the act of killing, defense, or construction that led to the concept of an axe.

To use analysis or synthesis alone penalizes us. It is possible to perform analysis as a pure intellectual activity (as in solving calculus equations), but the overall purpose of analysis by humans is to allow better synthesis. In analysis where unknowns and uncertainty are present, synthesis is necessary to adapt analytical techniques to the problem or, if necessary, to synthesize new analytical techniques. Synthesis is also benefited immeasurably by the use of analysis. Complex modern constructions such as large organizations, aircraft, sewage systems, or Christo's *Running Fence* could simply not be accomplished without analysis. It is, therefore, sad when those who identify themselves with the two problem solving approaches become antagonists. The painter and the applied mathematician, the poet and the chemist, the singer and the engineer should rely on a balance of analysis and synthesis, but they can often be found preaching the virtues of one to the exclusion of the other. This is always a loss, since the combination of the two is essential for creativity and reasonable change in complex situations.

CONVERGENCE-DIVERGENCE

Convergent thinking focuses on an answer. Long division is a simple example, as is calculating your income tax. Techniques are used that eliminate uncertainty, simplify complexity, and enhance decision-making ability. Much of education is convergent. Certainly you expect the thinking of experts to be convergent. You would like your doctor to converge to a diagnosis, your architect to converge to a design, your auto mechanic to converge to a solution, and members of your family to converge to a few important problems for you to help them with. Techniques such as trigonometry, sentence-parsing, decision analysis, double-entry bookkeeping, TV repair, and recipes for French bread are all convergent.

Divergent thinking refers to the process of generation of ideas, concepts, and approaches. It is an extremely powerful process and is perhaps less familiar because less emphasis is placed on it in our schools and public consciousness. It is possible to radically increase divergent thinking in problem solving. To the extent that more concepts are generated, decision making becomes more complicated. However, more alternates result in a greater probability of a better solution. Certainly more alternates are likely to permit a more creative solution, since initial concepts tend to be closely related to tradition.

Once again, the competent problem solver or problem-solving group should be able to handle both modes of thinking well and, in fact, in most problem-solving activities there is an overlap. It is inefficient merely to continue to generate ideas with no accompanying convergent thinking, as the pool will grow to a size that will make decision making nearly impossible. Similarly, it is foolish to converge without spending some effort to ensure that alternates have been at least examined, if not consciously generated. However, once again we find individuals, groups, and even organizations identifying only with the divergent (blue-sky, creative, idea person) or the convergent (tough-minded, decisive, practical). We find engineering schools obsessed with convergence and art schools obsessed with divergence, even though as a practitioner in one and at least a dabbler in the other, I do not find the difference in intellectual activities between the sculptor and the machine designer that great. As in the previous cases, separation by specialty is a loss, especially in situations requiring creativity and change.

DEDUCTION-INDUCTION

Deduction and induction are another way of slicing the pie. Deduction has to do with reasoning from the general to the specific. It is usually associated with analysis, but this can be misleading. We use it to go from a theory to specific facts or from an equation to an answer. We use it a lot in school and when we are applying a technique. We expect that great detectives, such as Sherlock Holmes, use it because their overall knowledge is so scientific and complete that they can deduce the criminal in specific cases.

Induction, on the other hand, is reasoning from the specific to the general. It is the way that scientific theories are created and how we often solve problems. In most of life, adequate theory does not exist. We try to figure out the problem (and the answer) from observing specific shortcomings. Induction does not have as much mystique as deduction in our society because it does not seem as "right-answer" oriented as deduction. In that sense, it falls in with synthesis and divergent thinking. However, we rely upon it a great deal, especially in creativity and change. Competent problem solving requires both specializations.

FREUD AND HIS PERSONALITY TYPES

Sigmund Freud thought that people go through a chronological series of stages in growing older. Table 6-2 outlines these stages of development in the male. In the first two stages, fixation refers to a lingering attachment to the behavior of the previous stage. Reaction formation is a process that allows a conflict to be resolved by reacting in opposition to urges. In other words, if we will not let go of our side of the conflict, we fixate. If we give up and accept the other side, we form a reaction. Hopefully we do neither and move on to the next conflict.

Freud thought that we retain various characteristics acquired during this developmental period. The characteristics most usually referred to are the top four on the right-hand side of the table. The oral character has an overpowering need for psychological and physical input from others. The reactor from the oral stage, who is the antisocial loner, disclaims a need for others and antagonizes those

TABLE 6-2 Freud's Stages of Psychosexual Development in the Male

Stage	Approximate age	Main characteristics of that period	Consequences
Oral	1	Stimulation of mouth (sucking; later: biting, chewing)	Fixation → "Oral character" (passive, dependent) Reaction-formation → Vehement denial of dependence (tough, sarcastic, etc.)
Anal	1–3	Pleasurable stimulation of bowels. Later: requirement to control this pleasure during toilet training	Fixation → Disorderly, tempestuous Reaction-formation → "Anal character" (compulsively orderly, stingy, obstinate)
Phallic	3–5	Stimulation of genitals, as in infantile masturbation →	Oedipus complex ↓ Sexual desire directed toward mother ↓ Hostility and fear of father ↓ Renunciation of mother, identification with father ↓ Formation of superego
Latency	6–13	Sexuality repressed	
Genital	Puberty on	Rearousal of sexuality →	Sexual desire with interest in partner's erotic and social satisfaction: love

he or she meets. The person fixed at the anal stage is a troublemaker living out his behavior on the toilet-training seat. Finally, the anal-compulsive character (also frequently mentioned in creativity litera-ture) resolves conflict by tightening up rather than loosening. The anal-compulsive individual refuses to give up his or her feces — taking on socially symbolic behavior such as a high degree of clean-liness and orderliness, obstinacy, and stinginess.

Whether we believe Freud's theories or not, we certainly know people who fit into his stereotypes; the person with unusual needs for others, the lone wolf, the troublemaker, and people who persist in organizing not only themselves, but also the world around them. We also have experience with their behavior in problem solving. The person who will not make a move for fear of displeasing others, the person who will not work with others, the person who seems to gain visibility by sabotaging the effort, and the person who will not accept the unknown. Although these personality categories are usually used with reference to latent stages and their negative impact, they can also be used to point out certain characteristics in problem-solving groups.

JUNG AND THE MYERS-BRIGGS TEST

As a final set of specialties (this time more than two), let us look at the theories of Carl Jung, a contemporary of Freud's whose work is most easily understood by reading his book *Man and His Symbols*. He described people in terms of dichotomies of behavior. Four of these that are central to problem solving are introvert-extrovert, sensory-intuitive, thinking-feeling, and judgmental-perceptive. Introvert-ex-trovert refers to whether one would rather create and optimize so-lutions within one's own mind as an intellectual challenge (introvert) or whether one would rather solve problems and implement the solutions in the world (extrovert). The introvert is happiest wrestling with studies, enigmas, and complex situations that challenge his or her intellectual ability. The researcher is an example. The extrovert is happier organizing people and other resources to better accomplish results. The operations manager is a typical example.

Sensory people prefer to rely upon their senses to gather data — to observe, measure, read, ask experts. Intuitive people tend to rely upon information that is already in their memory. The sensory person may distrust his or her intuition if it conflicts with the "facts." The intuitive person distrusts the facts if they conflict with intuition. The thinking person prefers to make decisions by logically extrapolating from data, whatever its source. The feeling person prefers to rely upon his or her "gut" feelings and to make decisions according to emotional messages. The thinking person is likely to distrust feelings, and the feeling person tends to distrust facts and logic. A prospective house-buyer who is a thinker will probably not buy a house he or she loves if there is sufficient question about future housing values of neighborhood conditions. A house-buyer who is a feeling person will probably make the purchase.

The last dichotomy has to do with the judgmental style of the problem solver. One side represents the judgmental person who is sure of his or her stand (for example, the person who knows the relative value of nuclear energy and welfare). On the other side is the so-called "perceptive" person, who tends to adapt to the situation. Such a person is likely to be influenced by well-presented views of nuclear energy from opposing sides and to see both the good and the bad of welfare.

Problem solving requires all of these attributes. Certainly it is helpful to brood on problems within the mind in order to come up with more elegant and clever solutions. However, it is important to implement solutions if the problem-solving activity is to be meaningful. It is important to be sensitive to data as well as to the capability of the mind to integrate complex situations and respond with a "hunch." Analysis and respect for information is as essential in making good decisions as is sensitivity to the feelings of others and confidence in one's own course as evidenced through the emotions. Finally, judgment is necessary to come to conclusions, but a perceptive approach is valuable in being able to deal with options. Once again, representatives of the extremes often march under different flags. The assembly plant manager and the theoretical physicist, the technician performing experiments on an automobile engine and the painter following messages from within, the stock market analyst and the occasional Las Vegas gambler, the board chairman and the college sophomore certainly are stereotypes of different styles and probably would clash over values and problem-solving styles. They may not even get along very well. However, they each have something to contribute and to offer each other. The person who is strongly extrovert-sensory-thinking-judgmental certainly sounds like a left-brain thinker, might be expected to be an intellectual battering ram, and in fact is often found in management in traditional companies in traditional roles. The person who is introvert-intuitive-feeling-perceptive might be expected to be a right-brain thinker capable of a high degree of creativity and needing careful nurturing and support. To the extent that these styles do not come together, we lose important input, especially in situations involving creativity and change.

How would you rank yourself in the general population according to Jung's four dichotomies? Where do you think your spouse and children would rank you? How about your coworkers and your boss? These dichotomies are the foundation for the widely used Myers-Briggs Type Inventory. The test utilizes 126 questions to rank the test-taker in the population. The test is, in turn, the basis of the popular book *Please Understand Me* written by David Kiersey and Marilyn Bates.

In one of the summer executive programs run by the Stanford Graduate School of Business, participants were sent the Myers-Briggs test before the program. When they arrive they received the usual large plastic name tag that contained not only their name, but also their Myers-Briggs score. They were then put in groups to work on problems and very rapidly learned to take account of the problem-solving style of others in the group. I do the same thing in my classes and have done the same thing with many kinds of professionals. Given a framework to emphasize and organize cognitive styles, people are smart enough to use them.

There are other problem-solving specialties, of course, and ways to measure many of them, although there is no universal instrument that can totally describe an individual, a group, or a large organization. However, for our purpose, we do not need the perfect instrument. We merely must keep in mind that humans are specialized and that these specialties can be described. To the extent that individuals, groups, or organizations cling too closely to a particular specialty, they fall into a rut, useful when the road is going where we wish to go and harmful when we wish to go elsewhere. To the extent that we are willing to take advantage of these specialties, we can combine them into new intellectual constructs, capable of increased creativity and responsiveness to change.

7

Overcoming Ruts
and Boxes

You have now been introduced to some rudiments of problem solving. You've thought about the unconscious, how the brain and nervous system works, how information is stored, and the positive and negative roles of our intellectual programming. Along the way we have discussed methods of increasing creativity and change. We are now going to shift our focus to larger issues — how to provide the environment and wherewithal to increase personal and organizational creativity. We accomplish part of this by becoming aware of the process and spending the necessary effort to consciously augment our business-as-usual problem-solving habits. However, there is more.

Before we look at these larger issues, let us discuss creativity techniques. These techniques are intended to result in the production of concepts that deviate from the usual. They are the focus of a number of books on creativity as well as many workshops and short courses given on the topics of creativity and change. Creativity techniques are popular among authors and teachers because they can be described and conveyed much more easily than the more general concerns we are discussing in this book. They are popular among customers, clients, and readers because of their apparent simplicity.

There is universal demand for creativity "pills" — for nine or five or better yet three rules for creativity. The most popular prescription to sell to managers seeking the means to increase creativity is a relatively small list of these techniques, each with a "bullet" in front. I know, since I am very reluctant to dispense such prescriptions, even though they bring a high price.

I do not mean to sound negative concerning creativity and change techniques oriented toward the production of new concepts. As a matter of fact, they usually work. None of them are universal. Problem solving being what it is, no single technique is optimal for everyone. When I first became interested in creativity in the 1950s there was an abundance of creativity techniques floating around. Since I find such things fascinating, I learned a large number of them. However, unfortunately (or perhaps fortunately), I discovered that use of these techniques does not fit my natural problem-solving process. I personally get more value from the generalizations underlying these techniques. However, many people find specific techniques more useful and most people seem to like them. They generally accomplish the purpose of inducing unusual and, therefore, potentially creative concepts. They also add to the understanding of creative problem solving.

Unfortunately, more than just reading about them is necessary. As we mentioned, reading a memory book without spending the effort to learn the new structures does us no good other than the general entertainment we may derive from reading it. This is the case with creativity techniques. If they are to do us any good, we must practice them until they become a natural component of our problem solving.

My main problem with creativity techniques has to do with their obsession with ideation (the production of ideas). In fact, individuals, groups, and organizations have ideas without these techniques and, if their idea production is inadequate, it is not too difficult to increase both quantity and quality. It is in support of these ideas and implementation that creativity usually stumbles, and most creativity techniques are less successful at overcoming the problems of resource allocation, living with risk, and continual selling that are involved in implementation.

However, all that aside, let us discuss some creativity techniques. Even if they are not by themselves the key to creative output, they certainly lead one to a better understanding of how the mind works and are examples of specific application of the material discussed in the earlier chapters to creative problem solving. They all result in effort being focused in new directions. However, they also modify the usual habitual process of problem solving. They break "set."

CHECKLISTS

Checklists simply require us to consciously control our thinking in order to cover alternates that our unconscious might ignore in order to simplify our life. We are all familiar with the type of checklist we take to the grocery store. The type we are discussing here reminds us to think a wide variety of thoughts. One of the better known and more elegant is the one presented by George Polya in his classic book *How to Solve It*. Polya is a mathematician who happens to be quite interested in the process of problem solving. His list is presented here:

Understanding the Problem

What is the unknown? What are the data? What is the condition? Is it possible to satisfy the condition? Is the condition sufficient to determine the unknown? Or is it insufficient? Or redundant? Or contradictory? Draw a figure. Introduce suitable notation. Separate the various parts of the condition. Can you write them down?

Devising a Plan

Have you seen it before? Or have you seen the same problem in a slightly different form? Do you know a related problem? Do you know a theorem that could be useful? Look at the unknown. Try to think of a familiar problem having the same or a similar unknown.

Here is a problem related to yours and solved before. Could you use it? Could you use its method? Should you introduce some auxiliary element in order to make its use possible? Could you restate the problem? Could you restate it still differently? Go back to definitions.

If you cannot solve the proposed problem try to solve first some related problem. Could you imagine a more accessible related problem? A more general problem? A more special problem? An analogous problem? Could you solve a part of the problem? Keep only a part of the condition, drop the other part: how far is the unknown then determined, how can it vary?

Could you derive something useful from the data? Could you think of other data appropriate to determine the unknown? Could you change the unknown or the data, or both, if necessary, so that the new unknown and the new data are nearer to each other? Did you use all the data? Did you use the whole condition? Have you taken into account all essential notions involved in the problem?

Carrying Out the Plan

Carrying out your plan of the solution, check each step. Can you see clearly that the step is correct? Can you prove that it is correct?

Examining the Solution Obtained

Can you check the result? Can you check the argument? Can you derive the result differently? Can you see it at a glance? Can you use the result of the method for some other problem?

Even though Polya is a mathematician, his list obviously applies to other problems. It should be said once again that creativity techniques are not universal. I used to teach a class on problem solving to which I would invite two famous mathematicians. I would ask them to talk about the way in which they did mathematics. The reason for inviting these two was that one used check lists in his approach, was quite impressed by Polya's book, and was most methodical in his approach to research. The other had no idea of how he did mathematics, was not particularly impressed by Polya's list, and relied much more on faith in the "aha" following long periods of thinking about problems and living his life.

The following checklist was contained in a book entitled *Applied Imagination* written by Alex Osborne, the Osborne in Batton, Barton, Durson, and Osborne, and published in 1953.

Checklist for New Ideas

Put to Other Uses?
New ways to use as is? Other uses if modified?
Adapt?
What else is like this? What other idea does this suggest? Does past offer a parallel? What could I copy? Whom could I emulate?
Modify?
New twist? Change meaning, color, motion, sound, odor, form, shape? Other changes?
Magnify?
What to add? More time? Greater frequency? Stronger? Higher? Longer? Thicker? Extra value? Plus ingredient? Duplicate? Multiply? Exaggerate?
Minify?
What to subtract? Smaller? Condensed? Miniature? Lower? Shorter? Lighter? Omit? Streamline? Split up? Understate?
Substitute?
Who else instead? What else instead? Other ingredient? Other material? Other process? Other power? Other place? Other approach? Other tone of voice?
Rearrange?
Interchange components? Other pattern? Other layout? Other sequence? Transpose cause and effect? Change pace? Change schedule?

Reverse?

Transpose positive and negative? How about opposites? Turn it backward? Turn it upside down? Reverse roles? Change shoes? Turn tables? Turn other cheek?

Combine?

How about a blend, an alloy, an assortment, an ensemble? Combine units? Combine purposes? Combine appeals? Combine ideas?

Although I claim not to rely too strongly on checklists, being more interested in the underlying cognitive and behavioral reasons for certain types of problem solving, it has occasionally been pointed out to me that I use checklists anyway. The organization of my book *Conceptual Blockbusting*, is a type of checklist in that it offers a categorization of common mental blocks to creativity (perceptual, emotional, cultural, environmental, intellectual, and expressive). In a way, the outline of this book follows a personal checklist I use in my consulting (awareness of process? techniques? resources? reward system? management style? decision making? strategy?). I had my unconscious use of checklists pointed out to me in a particularly strong way in conjunction with a talk I gave to some managers of Spectraphysics on the topic of creativity. The person who had arranged the talk wanted a checklist. I did not cooperate in giving him one. However, he managed to talk me out of one by sending me his version of the topics I would cover, which I of course corrected. When I arrived to give my talk I found everyone happily drinking coffee out of a cup with my "checklist" on it. What could I say? It was one of my more successful talks because people could look at their cup and figure out what I was trying to say. Figure 7-1 shows the cup (and the list).

ATTRIBUTE ANALYSIS

Another approach to set-breaking is through a process called attribute analysis. This has to do with breaking our propensity to operate at the highest possible level of generalization. Often, if we consider the attributes of people, things, situations, or whatever, we can come to different conclusions than if we operate with our stereotypes. Suppose, for example, that we were back attempting to list possible uses for ordinary yellow wooden pencils (remember the end of Chapter 1?). We could list the attributes of pencils. They are hexagonal, pointed, made of wood, painted yellow, equipped with a rubber eraser on the end, and so on. We could probably list a large number of these if we became concerned with the nature of the paint and

FIGURE 7-1 The Checklist Cup

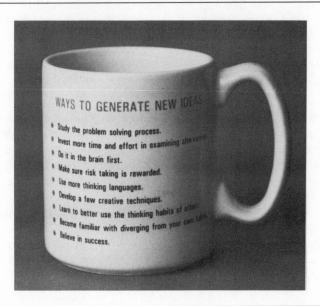

other esoterica. We could then take one attribute, such as being made of wood, and list what the attributes of wood are: it burns, floats, insulates against electricity, has structural ability, etc. We could then take one of these, such as "floats," and create a list of what floats: canoes, life preservers, aircraft carriers, toilet floats, etc. (You like using pencils for making aircraft carriers and toilet floats?). If we were only so good as to come up with ten original attributes, ten at the next level, and ten uses for each of these, we would have an instant one thousand uses for a pencil. If we went to one hundred each time, we would have a cool million. Needless to say, few of these would be very practical but, after all, the game was the length of the list.

There are other set-breakers. A famous scientist named Fritz Zwicky made use of a technique he called "morphological analysis." In this technique, he would choose parameters of importance. As a simple example, if he were trying to think of a new concept in personal transportation, he might choose the motive power source, the type of passenger support, and the medium in which the vehicle operates. He might then list all of the alternate possibilities he could think of for each of these parameters. He would then examine all possible combinations for interest. Figure 7-2 shows such a situation graphically.

We find, for instance, that one intersection in this figure represents a steam-driven system that runs on rails and has passengers in chairs. This is not very interesting because trains exist. So do systems driven by electricity that sling people from cables (ski lifts) and gasoline-powered ones that seat people and travel on hard surfaces. However, how about pneumatic-powered ones in which people lie down and are transported through tubes or gravity-powered ones in which people stand and are transported down a belt? Like attribute listing, this technique has the ability to create large numbers of options. If one chose six parameters and generated ten alternates for each, one would have once again one million options. By using a computer, one could easily generate more possible combinations than one could ever consider. A good technique for Zwicky, we must assume, but not necessarily for everyone.

An interesting combination of attribute analysis and morphological analysis is a technique contained in Koberg and Bagnalls' book *The Universal Traveler.* The rules are:

FIGURE 7-2 A Morphological Analysis of a New Concept in Personal Transportation

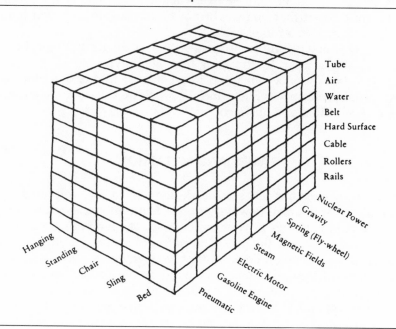

1. List the attributes of the situation.
2. Below each attribute, place as many alternates as you can think of.
3. When completed, make many random runs through the alternates, picking up a different one from each column and assembling the combinations into entirely new forms of your original subject.

EXAMPLE: Improve a ballpoint pen

ATTRIBUTES			
Cylindrical	Plastic	Separate Cap	Steel Cartridge
ALTERNATES			
Faceted	Metal	Attached cap	No cartridge
Square	Glass	No cap	Permanent
Beaded	Wood	Retracts	Paper cartridge
Sculptured	Paper	Cleaning cap	Ink cartridge

INVENTION: A cube pen — one corner writes, leaving six faces for ads, calendars, photos, etc. It might look like the drawing in Figure 7-3. You might not be overwhelmed with this invention, but you must admit that you might not be too surprised if you found one some day on a motel desk.

The message behind techniques such as attribute and morphological analysis is clear. By dropping from stereotypes down to specific characteristics we jog our mind into behavior that is different than our usual problem solving, which is predicated upon a higher level of generalization and abstraction.

GAMES AND METAPHORS

There are other approaches to set-breaking, of course. You can design gimmicks for yourself (always a good idea) that cause you to divert the usual happenings in your mind. A simple one I originally heard from George Prince, the president of Synectics Inc., in Boston, was the tactic of opening a book, putting your finger blindly on a word, and then attempting to use that word in the process of finding a concept. For instance, you want to figure out a way to get exercise more pleasantly? Open a book and put your finger on a word. The word is *hinge* (I just did it). How can you get exercise more pleasantly using the concepts involved in the word *hinge*? Think about it a while.

FIGURE 7-3 A Cube Pen

I don't know if you will succeed, but you will certainly break your mental set.

Bob Lavelle, the editor of this book, was a tremendous joy to work with because he became totally involved in it. Among other contributions, he did all of the exercises and sent me his experiences. In this one, he thought of the following:

1. Attach a ring with stretch handles over the knob of the hinge of a door and exercise by pulling on the handles while watching TV.
2. Attach counterweights to your refrigerator door. Every time you go to eat, you exercise.
3. Using a series of hinges, weights, and pulleys, construct your own Nautilus-type machine that, with slow positive pressure as you lift a weight, turns the pages of a book. The machine is timed so

that it takes you long enough to lift the weight to read the page in front of you.

Another approach to set-breaking is the use of metaphor. One of the more articulate and long-time advocates for the use of metaphor is W. J. J. Gordon of Synetics Educational Systems Inc. In his early book *Synectics*, Gordon talks about the use of four types of metaphor that can be used to encourage original concepts and approaches: personal analogy, direct analogy, symbolic analogy, and fantasy analogy. The personal analogy requires that the problem solver identify with part or all of the problem and its solution. The direct analogy attempts to solve a problem by the direct application of parallel facts, knowledge, technology, or whatever. The symbolic analogy is somewhat like the personal analogy, except that the identification is between the problem and objective and impersonal objects or images. The fantasy analogy allows the problem solver to use fantasy to solve problems. All of these approaches used the information stored in memory in new combinations in order to realize new concepts.

PROBLEM DEFINITION

Let us now move to a topic that is given all too little consideration in problem solving — the definition of the problem itself. One of the many ways in which our mind attempts to make our life easier is to solve the first impression of the problem that it encounters. This first impression, of course, is not only dependent on the incoming information, but also on the experience and the intellectual biases of the problem solver.

I have done a great deal of consulting on problems ranging from professional (electromechanical design, management of change and creativity) to personal (sophomores, good friends in the midst of divorces). I think that the greatest service I have provided in most of these instances is to allow people to think about their problem. When forced to communicate their problem to me, they usually do so much flailing about that they end up with a different view of their problem than they had when they began. Such is the arbitrariness of our perception of problems. In my book *Conceptual Blockbusting*, I told the traumatic tale of my early involvement in the development of a mechanism that was not needed. Since then, the same thing has happened to me many times.

People gain weight and see their problem as getting enough exercise to get back in shape (perhaps they are eating too much and never were the physical paragons they remember). They claim to have divorced an anal-compulsive type and married another (perhaps there is no one "healthy" enough to live in their state of disorganization). They focus their lives to make a lot of money and find that they wanted respect from people who do not give business people high marks. They direct the efforts of their company on the development of a new product to augment the one that is not selling well and find that the problem is lack of marketing ability, not the product. They pump iron to build muscle to impress the pom-pom girl, who just happens to be bored to tears with muscle.

Such happenings are the stuff of life. Why? Because we do not think very hard about just exactly why things are not working the way we wish they would. We pick the most obvious (to us) shortcoming and set to work on it. In doing so, we are embarrassingly casual about the directions implicit in the wording of the problem. Supposing I am becoming annoyed by the increasing traffic in the area in which I live. Suppose, further, that I decide to do something about it. Just imagine the different directions I might take from the following problem statements:

1. The population is expanding too rapidly.
2. There are too many people in the area.
3. There are too many cars in the area.
4. The traffic flow in the area makes no sense.
5. I am tired of driving in all of the traffic around here.
6. This area is getting to be a hassle.
7. Driving is no fun anymore.

Just think of the difference between "There are too many cars in the area," "There are too many cars in the US," and "There are too many cars on El Camino Real."

Many approaches to increasing creativity demand analysis of the problem statement and perhaps encourage the confrontation of alternate statements. Often the problem as given is misleading as far as efficient improvement of the situation is concerned. The problem statement may also be too specific. It is foolish to fail to spend some mental energy rephrasing a problem in both more global and more specific ways. The reason is simple: *more specific problem statements lead to quicker solutions but less conceptual creativity than more general statements.* Think of the difference between the problem of environmental pollution and the problem of dog droppings on your lawn. Consider the difference between the problem of transporting your kids to school and keeping them dry when they ride their bicycles in the rain; the difference between cutting the costs of your railroads and making a profit in the transportation business; the difference between developing a competitive personal computer and establishing a profitable niche in the information business.

EDUCATION AND PROBLEM SOLVING

Another way to break set is to expand the connections between memory files through plain old education. Education has two roles. One has to do with learning new information, techniques, and attitudes. These things are often necessary in creativity and change situations. It is not unusual for individuals to return to school or go in search of self-teaching material in these situations. It is also not unusual for organizations to set up training and educational programs. However, education has still another and important long-term role. It can cause us to question our assumed mental limits. If in fact we turned away from poetry in high school and then take a poetry course in our midforties, we might receive an interesting and provocative message. We are, in fact, not incompetent at something we gave ourself no credit for. This is the mind-expanding role of education, and it is a particularly valuable one. Most of us benefit from periodic reminders that we can learn new tricks if we work hard enough.

Unfortunately, we spend a large part of our original formal educations learning facts and techniques that are "required." During this time, we also come to overly firm and often erroneous conclusions as to what our abilities and weaknesses are. I am always fascinated by the sureness behind statements of college students such as "I am lousy at math," "I cannot draw," or "I am no good at literature." Such statements are usually based on school grades and often do not even reflect a true understanding of the nature of the intellectual disciplines. It is surely not uncommon for a college freshman to enroll in a very rapid calculus course that includes math, science, and engineering majors, get a C+ in the course, and conclude that they are "lousy at math" despite the fact that their high school SAT test placed them in the upper 10 percent of all college-bound seniors.

When we complete our formal education, we often carry these rather arbitrary conclusions about our abilities with us. We often strengthen them through time, as we discussed earlier. Additional education can modify these conclusions, add strengths, and broaden our self-confidence in our ability to play new and different intellectual games. This is especially true if the education is in areas in which we did not consider ourselves strong. Good examples of this can presently be seen in the migration of older (than traditional students) women to professional schools. However, it applies equally to all of us. If we take a creative writing or poetry course when we are forty-year-old managers, we learn a lot about poetry and probably find out that our antipoetry bias was false. We may have to admit that not only can we deal with poetry but probably a large number of other topics that we had thought were "off limits" to us. It is possible to find educational opportunities to reexamine almost every aspect of one's intellectual abilities. It is not only possible, but valuable. I think, for instance, that all engineers should take a course in marketing. I do not think that they should do this so that they can become marketing professionals, but rather because engineers have such completely different viewpoints and philosophies from marketing people.

Education is necessary in specific creativity and change situations in order to provide new and pertinent knowledge, techniques, and attitudes either for direct application or to improve communication and decision making. However, an investment of time in education outside of one's traditional specialty or set of problem-solving habits pays great long-term dividends not only in broadening one's knowledge, technique, and attitude base, but also in recalibrating one's perception of intellectual limits. General education overcomes ruts and boxes.

8

Time, Money, and Creativity

As we remarked in the first chapter of this book, creativity requires perspiration. Our specialized brains and nervous systems, our un-conscious problem-solving habits, and our hierarchical information systems all make us admirably efficient when conducting business as usual but conspire against us when new directions are in the wind. In such situations, effort is required. The last chapter contained techniques of focusing effort in order to create original concepts. However, concepts are not enough. This chapter is concerned with resources necessary to carry concepts into reality.

It would be nice if creative problem solving needed fewer resources than solving our usual problems. Many individuals, groups, and organizations become interested in creativity when they are running out of resources. "I am having trouble making my house payments; I need to become creative." "My competition is taking away my market share and I am out of capital to develop new products; I need to become creative." I am sometimes called by companies who are running out of resources and then decide they need a creativity consultant. My usual response is that they should call the Pope and ask for a prayer. They need more than creativity. It is possible to look backwards in time and find people who have accomplished a great deal with few resources through brilliant and well-timed concepts. However, one should not rely upon such occurrences in the future in order to keep the wolf away from the door.

Perhaps the most difficult topic to discuss in conjunction with the management of creativity and change is that of resource allocation. Creativity is a word that tends to be used by people who want more for less. However, the most common reason for lack of individual creative accomplishment is simply unwillingness to allocate the resources. Successful novelists typically devote years to a work, and it is usually their main activity in life. If a professional novelist writes six hours a day and produces a book in three years, how long are you going to take if you write three hours a week? Even if you are as fast as a professional and able to remember your work between writing sessions, you are involved in a thirty-year writing project. Professionals do not complete novels in a few months worth of spare time while holding down a job and/or house with their main energy. Successful painters not only paint all of the time, but also devote their lives to the agony of attempting to express what they feel. They also buy good brushes, paint, and canvas. Many people I know try to be creative on the side. That is OK, unless one's expectations cause one to judge oneself according to world-class standards. If that is the case, one needs to allocate world-class resources to the task.

Resources are necessary to accomplish anything worthwhile, even in business as usual. However, when we talk about change and creativity, we are not just talking about resources. We are talking about the allocation of resources in an atmosphere of increased risk and decreased efficiency. As I said in the Introduction, I have seen no free lunches through creativity and no major changes accomplished without costs. In fact, the greater the desired creativity and the change, the proportionately larger should be the resource investment.

These resources are first of all necessary to cover the experimental nature of the venture — the probable wrong turns and unexpected complications. Second, something new must be taken to a high degree of completion if it is to compete with something old because the world as well as the innovator is programmed for business as usual. If I desire to become a world-class painter, I must invest the resources to communicate my message in a professional "painterly" way. In other words, I must pay the price of mastering technique. A business cannot expect a concept on paper to compete with an established product with a sales track record. In order to have any effect, concepts must be brought to something close to reality. This one-of-a-kind development is expensive and time-consuming. It is also uncertain.

In order to cover contingencies, resources allocated to new directions cannot simply be based on predicted problems, since unpredicted problems are sure to arrive. The only reasonable way to budget for these events is to use past experience in similar new developments. However, even then the uncertainties are such that often the budget will be inadequate both in money and time.

As an example of resource needs, let us look at the money used in industry to support the investigation of new directions. Each year, *Business Week* magazine publishes a study of some eight hundred publicly owned companies that have over $35,000,000 in sales and who spend at least $1,000,000 or 1 percent of sales on research and development. Table 8-1 lists the fifteen companies that spent the most on R&D expenditures from the 1985 article, along with some interesting indicators.

The information in the *Business Week* survey was compiled from data that companies submitted to the Securities and Exchange Commission. It does not necessarily give an overall measure of the actual availability and nature of resources for creativity and change. I have worked for a company in which resources were tightly controlled and allocated specifically to products and processes devoted to busi-

TABLE 8-1
The Fifteen Companies That Spent the Most on Research and Development in 1984

Company	Sales in Millions of Dollars	Profits in Millions of Dollars	R&D in Millions of Dollars	Percentage of Sales Dollars Spent on R&D	Dollars Per Employee Spent on R&D
IBM	45937	6582	3148	6.9	7971
General Motors	83890	4517	3076	3.7	4112
AT&T	53821	1370	2368	4.4	6488
Ford Motor	52366	2907	1915	3.7	4991
DuPont	35915	1431	1097	3.1	6953
General Electric	27947	2280	1038	3.7	3146
United Technology	16332	645	1012	6.2	4925
Eastman Kodak	10600	923	838	7.9	6764
Exxon	90854	5528	736	0.8	4907
Digital Equipment	5584	329	631	11.3	7368
Hewlett-Packard	6044	665	592	9.8	7220
Xerox	8792	376	561	6.4	5426
ITT	12701	303	520	4.1	2064
Dow Chemical	11418	549	507	4.4	10181
Boeing	10354	787	506	4.9	5441

ness as usual. It was impossible to experiment with any new direction without specific R&D funds. In companies such as these, the R&D expenses are a true indicator of the level of resources consumed. I have worked for another company in which R&D money was in fact used for short-term problem solving in conjunction with marketed items. In a company such as this R&D funding is misleading in that much of it is not "R" and barely "D". I have finally worked for a company (I, of course, loved it) where it was easy to try new things. If formal R&D money was not available, it was usually a simple thing to "bootleg" resources. In companies such as this, the formally budgeted R&D money is only a part of the resources allocated to creativity and change.

There are other problems with these figures, of course. They do not take into account the different budgeting patterns of different industries. Industries that are capital intensive (oil production) obviously show up differently than industries that are people intensive (computer software and services). Exxon, for instance, spent $4,907 per employee, even though they only spent 0.8 percent of their sales on R&D. ITT, on the other hand, spent 4.1 percent of their sales on R&D but only $2,064 per employee.

These difficulties with comparing R&D expenditures between companies, however, are not the point. The message is that the fifteen leading companies are extraordinarily successful companies and dedicate a very large amount of money to R&D.

RESOURCES FOR THE RIGHT PEOPLE

We have thus far been talking about the amount of resources necessary to explore new directions. However, this is not the only difficulty. The resources must be available to those in the company who have the problem. Is this an obvious statement? It may be, but not everyone understands it. As previously mentioned, resources for creativity and change are often budgeted with an eye toward tradition, the competition, and present success. However, problems can change. One hears a great deal in industry about the need for increased productivity and quality. In fact, I have been told by presidents of large companies that these are the major challenges facing industry in the United States today.

Much of the responsibility for increasing such things as quality and productivity is in the hands of process people (manufacturing, assembly, and testing). They are being expected to be clever, to be creative, and to change. How much R&D money do they have? Ask that question of manufacturing people and you will get initial incomprehension followed by tears. I recently was in a discussion about robots with a manufacturing manager who was responsible for a large operation. The best way to learn rapidly about robots is to buy one and start playing around with it. Robots are not that expensive by industry standards. However, this manager's budget apparently made it difficult for him to acquire one. If we want creativity and change in areas such as productivity and quality, people are going to have to experiment and will make some mistakes. They need equipment they do not now have and time to think. If these resources are not available, creativity and change will occur slowly, if at all. As problem areas change, the resources for creativity and change must follow.

TIME ENOUGH TO THINK

What about schedules? We are fortunately optimistic when it comes to looking at the future. This is partly due to the inability to predict all of the things that will go wrong. Over time we learn to use contingency factors, which may either be explicit or built into experience, but even then we can occasionally miss on the negative side, just as we occasionally miss on the positive. One must simply deal with schedule slippages as well as possible when they occur, because often they will.

I was employed for a while in planetary exploration during the early 1960s, when we were barely able to reach the planets. Due to the geometry of the solar system, it is only possible to journey to such planets as Mars and Venus every couple of years or so. In the early 1960s, there was an unrealistic expectation of the speed at which we were going to explore the planets fueled both by the perceived race with the Russians and by national eagerness. Technology was also advancing rapidly, so a two-year-old spacecraft was not that appealing. In essence, we could not miss our launch dates, and we did not. However, the resource cost paid was extraordinary. One would not like to pay such a cost in most personal or private competitive situations. One would rather balance cost with slippage. However, this requires an understanding of the reasons for and the reasonableness of slippages.

I have seen people tolerate unrealistic slippages. However, I have also seen people give up projects because of reasonable slippage and resort to scapegoats in the case of situations in which schedules were delayed by happenings that were almost in the category of acts of God. It is fun to watch what is sometimes called the defense business. Because of the advantage of technological superiority and the complexity of modern warfare, the military is extraordinarily good at asking for products that are unprecedented. Because of the way in which contracts are structured, technical optimism, and past successes, companies will bid aggressively for the privilege of producing these products. Schedules (and resources) then slip, and you are familiar with the press that results. The creativity and change involved in this work are great. Our ability to handle the resource and scheduling unknowns with reasonable equanimity are less. Let us say that ambivalence results. Is it mere incompetence that results in so many examples of budgets being exceeded and schedules being missed, or is some of it perhaps due to a lack of appreciation for the unknowns involved?

THE AMBIVALENCE OF BUDGETING

Ambivalence always accompanies the budgeting of resources for creativity and change. We often want creativity and change specifically because we are short on resources. A small company is successful enough to receive competition from a big one. As the big one tightens the screws, the small company at first assumes that the big company is too traditional and sluggish to harm it and tries to continue on its successful path. At some point things become bad enough, as recognized by shrinking profits, and the company embarks on a path of increasing creativity and change. However, by that time, resources are scarce, to say the least. The result is often the demise of the small company. Many examples of this can be seen in the computer business, where small, clever groups of people thought that the IBMs of the world just could not move fast enough.

Ambivalence may also occur because of the long-term nature of creativity and change as opposed to the short-term events of quarterly profits or monthly bills coming due. Even if our problem can be solved by creativity, we may not be able to solve it instantly. We may have to invest real resources in the short term in order to improve our situation in the future. We want a short-term improvement in "more for the buck" and end up with a short-term commitment of "bucks" to get to the desired end. As the short-term wisdom says, R&D comes out of profits (usually this quarter's profits).

For example, when a new computer system is purchased the desired effect, of course, is that efficiency will instantly increase and costs will drop. No way! First of all, employees unfamiliar with the system are pushed into experimentation. They must spend considerable time and effort learning to use the system. Not only must they learn to use it, but they must also become good enough at it so that their performance exceeds that under the old procedures. It is not enough to read the Wordstar manual. It is necessary that an employee become more proficient than he or she was using the typewriter before the profits emerge. During this learning period, it may become obvious that insufficient R&D was allocated, and impatience may then result.

The next discovery will be that information can be produced with the new system that looks interesting and worthwhile, but that could not realistically have been produced with the old. We have gone through a restful period of at least fifty years in which telephone budgets, the speed of mail, available filing cabinets and time, and available hours to compose and decode messages have constrained information. Computers have changed all of this. Now we can generate and save much more information than we could in the past and must rethink what information we need, in what form, and where. This is an extremely difficult job, and an organization with a new computer system will spend a large amount of its time and the time of those with whom they deal on this problem. Finally, the computer system will allow an increase of efficiency. However, even then it may not result in lower costs because the quality of the service may improve.

Similar trends occur in attempts to increase individual creativity and ability to respond to change. One may become serious about a creative hobby in order to achieve a better-balanced life and, therefore, bring more to one's job. However, the attraction of the hobby may become so strong that less time is spent on the job. One may decide that fashionable dress is a benefit in one's profession and end up investing large amounts of money and time in stores and less energy on one's profession.

We are now going to take a new direction in this book. The next chapter is concerned with the role of our culture and emotions in creativity. This is material that has been traditionally considered in the study of creativity. It is based upon psychological theory having to do with behavior rather than that concerned with thinking per se. It has to do with our feelings and will lead us to yet another set of conclusions and techniques having to do with increasing creativity and responsiveness to change.

9

Emotion, Risk, and Problem Solving

Emotions inevitably accompany creativity and change. You probably remember the emotions you experienced during the exercises that asked you to write a poem, design a lamp, and work a math problem. Some of these emotions are positive — excitement, fun, humor. Others are negative — embarrassment, fear, anxiety. Do the following exercise with a group of friends in order to experience both types of emotions. It requires that you deviate somewhat from your usual social behavior.

EXERCISE

This exercise involves creating the sound of a zoo. The table below assigns you an animal;

First letter of last name	Animal
A–F	Tropical bird
G–L	Lion
M–R	Ape
S–Z	Seal

Now select a partner (emotions are more apparent in a culture or in the presence of at least one other person). Look each other in the eyes and hold eye contact while you each make your animal sound loudly with your mouth for at least ten seconds.

What emotions did you experience during this simple deviation? Did you feel a mixture of humor and embarrassment? The exercise, although initially producing discomfort, most likely resulted in laughter. Probably no matter what your assignment, your animal turned out to be an ass.

Such emotions are powerful factors in problem solving. Humor is extremely positive in situations of creativity and change. It allows us to take more risk and accompanies insights and solutions. The embarrassment is valuable to us, in that it makes us avoid situations outside of our habits or programs; it keeps us in "safe" zones. However, it has a negative effect on the processes of creativity and change since it inhibits us from deviating. It keeps us from failing but also prevents us from experimenting.

Creativity and change are risky, and these negative emotions are attempts to protect us from the unknown. When heading into the unknown, anything may happen — including failure. It takes courage and confidence to pursue new directions. It is important, when trying to be more creative, that we take risk and these negative emotions into account. There are ways to handle them intelligently. We can, first of all, understand them. Most of us find risk easier to live with if we understand and confront it, if we face the possible bad news directly and thereby become specific about what psychiatrists call generalized anxiety. We can also protect ourselves and others from risk by ensuring that failures will not result in unacceptable damage. Finally, we can reward ourselves and others for living with it. This chapter and the next will discuss risk and its management in creativity and change.

FEAR OF FAILURE

Failure is not pleasant. We are punished in many ways for it. First of all, we may have to lower our own self-image — a painful process. Second, others may think less of us. Third, we may gain less economic reward and political status than if we succeed. Finally, we may find that the world becomes less eager to support us in future endeavors. We know this well, so we do not like to fail.

However, most of us fear failure perhaps more than we should. Undoubtedly you have failed at things and found that not only have you survived, but also you have later chalked up the loss as a positive event in your life. This is often the viewpoint of those who have been divorced or who have failed in business. I have even had people who have been wounded in combat extol the virtues of combat to me. Certainly we tend to fear small failures more than we should. Most of us are more stable in our maturity than we think we are. A mistake or two are not going to affect us in a major way. However, we have been socialized to avoid all failure. We are, if you will, chicken.

Let us consider a couple of simple exercises having to do with risk. The first has to do with odds. We might assume that we would be interested in wagers with somewhat even odds, but this is not the case.

EXERCISE

Assume a simple world in which there are no taxes. Would you wager next year's income double or nothing on the toss of a fair coin? That is a fair bet. If you call the toss correctly, you receive twice your next year's income. If you call it incorrectly, you receive nothing.

Most of us would not take this wager because we know the real cost of no income next year (tuition payments, mortgages, food, etc.). I do not argue with this; I merely mention this wager to illustrate that, to most of us, a loss looms larger than an equivalent gain. We can compare these two a little more specifically. I could bribe you to take the bet in the exercise. Suppose I offered you a sum equal to your next year's income to play. Then if you called the toss correctly you would win three times next year's income and if you called it incorrectly you would receive one times next year's income. Better? Now let's drop back and see how big a bribe would be necessary to get you to play. Would you play for a 10 percent bribe? That would mean a win would be 210 percent of next year's salary and a loss would bring you 10 percent of next year's salary. How about a bribe of 20 percent? 30 percent? 40 percent? How high would the bribe have to be? Most responsible, mature people would want a bribe of somewhere between 60 percent and 100 percent of next year's salary before they would play. We seem to want about two-thirds of our income guaranteed before we will risk the remainder on a coin toss.

E X E R C I S E

This game has to do with a farming choice in a simple world. Imagine that you are a farmer and have a choice of one of three crops to plant. You must plant all of your land in the crop you choose. There are three possible conditions for the weather next year: perfect, acceptable, and lousy. Each is equally likely, and you cannot predict which will occur. The gains and losses for each crop and weather condition are shown in the following table.

	Weather		
	Perfect	*Acceptable*	*Lousy*
Crop #1	12	0	−3
Crop #2	6	3	0
Crop #3	3	3	3

Which would you plant? Crop #1? Crop #2? Crop #3?

The gains and losses are carefully rigged to eliminate decision theory, since the expected value of the gain from each crop is the same. Few people would plant the first crop. It appeals to the high-rollers, who look at the gain of 12 (million dollars, lollipops, giant steps, or whatever) and go for it. Most of us do not like the loss all that much. Crop #2 is the most popular choice. It looks like it has a reasonable correlation with weather, and the worse we can do is not make anything. Crop #3 appeals to people who like to sleep soundly and to pessimists who feel that since they are going to lose they should go for the crop involving the least loss.

RISK ANALYSIS

The reason I eliminated decision theory (to be discussed in Chapter 12) from the last exercise was to put you in a position where your feelings dictated the choice. These days one often encounters an analytical approach to managing risk. In such an approach, one attempts to predict failure modes, their importance, and the proba-bility of their occurring. This analysis enables one to approach the handling of risk in a more rational way. Resources can be allocated to prevent the more likely and critical failures, and a better sense of the potential for failure can be gained. Similar analysis has long been done in aerospace systems design and is becoming more widely used in fields such as environmental management, safety, and transportation. It removes some of the uncertainty by uncovering relationships and subdividing complex problems into manageable pieces.

It is also helpful in confronting risk. Many of us are more courageous if we analyze possible failures in detail. Quit my job and start a business? Risky! What might go wrong? I might neglect my spouse and kids and lose my family. The stress might destroy my health. I could even die from a heart attack. What if I failed? I might lose everything I own — my house, car, credit rating, confidence, reputation, and the respect of my friends. When I walked down the street in my ragged clothes little children would laugh and dogs would snarl at me. However, I probably would not have a heart attack. In fact, probably everything would not go wrong. I'll do it!

Risk analysis, however, is not able to remove all unknowns. Things continue to fail and people continue to act unpredictably. Creativity and change necessarily result in feelings of insecurity and uncertainty that cannot be totally controlled by cognitive techniques. Our emotions try to keep us away from possible failures, not draw us toward them.

FREUD AND CREATIVITY

Freudian theory is used a great deal in understanding the emotions involved with creativity and has been the basis of a great deal of writing on creativity and change. Let us consider the theory to see what it has to do with animal sounds and such. Freud saw the basis of our conflicts as the struggle between three subcomponents of our personality: the id, the ego, and the superego. The id is the most primitive and animal-like of these subcomponents. It is the home of all basic biological urges, such as the desire for sexual gratification, food and drink, elimination, and physical comfort. It is unconscious and insistent. The newborn baby is essentially all id, as is Garfield the cat. The id is insensitive to reality, to others, or to concepts of self. It is a grand itch that seeks to drive us headlong into scratching. It wants us to eat that cheesecake, make love to that person, take off those tight shoes, and urinate *now*. If we were to make an analog between problem solving and behavior, it contains our unsolved problems and our desire to solve them.

The ego is reality and is formed through experiences in the world. As the newborn seeks to follow the urges of the id, obstacles are met. Cries of hunger do not immediately bring the bottle, so the desire to eat cannot be filled immediately. Later, the pleas of the bowel cannot be answered except in a special, rather uncomfortable, room. Still later, sexual activities must be tailored to avoid too much disapproval from others. As the child attempts to satisfy the id's urges and meets with various degrees of acceptance or rejection, he or she slowly builds a complex system of behavior that is driven by the id but that is aware of the structures in which these desires can most practically be satisfied. Its unique characteristics say a lot about our uniqueness as individuals. If the id is the itch, the ego constrains our scratching to the constraints of the world about us. It wants us to solve our problems in practical ways.

However, we also have a superego. Many urgings of the id can be answered in a way that is consistent with the ego. If we are hungry for sweets and can reach the cookie jar (practicality), we can take a cookie. However, when we become older we may not do so, even though we can reach it and are hungry for a sweet. Something inside us tells us that taking a cookie is a no-no. This is the superego, which takes the place of all of those other physical constraints and watchful parents that surround us in our earlier years. The superego is our moral judge or conscience. It is developed by internalizing strongly held parental and social values. It tells us whether practical ways of satisfying our id are "good" or "bad." It does not like us to fail in the eyes of those whom we value.

Freud thought that much of the contents of our superego come from our parents, and that constraints are handed down from generation to generation and are unconscious and irrational. His model of the personality was like a sandwich, with a conscious and rational ego squeezed between two irrational portions — the id, prodding us relentlessly in all sort of directions, and the superego, telling us that some of the practical solutions worked out by the ego are better than others. He also emphasized that we are born with id and develop ego and superego very early in our life; the conflict between the urges of our id and the constraints placed upon us are instrumental in developing our personality. These patterns dictate the directions we take and the constraints we accept for the rest of our lives. They can also steer us into untenable situations.

Viewing problem solving in a Freudian light gives us a different perspective than the more cognitive approach stressed in the early part of this book. Solutions from the id must endure the judgment of the practical ego and the self-conscious superego. We reject not only the impractical, but also that which conflicts with our social and cultural values. I have strong urges to escape typing on this book. I have practical solutions as to how to do this. However, something keeps me working away in my stuffy room. You may become so miffed at a competitor that you would like to drive him or her out of business. Your ego, hearing this desire, can probably even accept some of your practical methods of accomplishing this. However, your superego is likely to say no.

The Freudian model certainly gives us confidence that the solutions to our problems are acceptable and implementable. However, what does it say about creativity and change? The ego constrains answers to regions of practicality but may keep us from a useful direction of thought. Relaxing our sense of practicality can allow fresh and profitable lines of thinking to emerge. The same is true of relaxing the superego, since ideas that are socially unacceptable might lead to others that are socially quite reasonable. Fortunately, as we will see later, both the ego and the superego can be relaxed.

Unless we do something to relax these subcomponents of our personality, they do not want us to consider things that may not be viable or to play fast and loose with our identity. They do not want us to play with risk. New ideas and directions are always risky because until proven over time we cannot be sure that they will be successful. Our egos and superegos therefore have trouble with them.

Freudian theory dwells heavily on the concept of anxiety, which is an emotional state akin to physical fear. Anxiety is unpleasant and so we attempt to avoid it by avoiding acts that could cause it, including risky ones. A good example of this fear of failure is writer's block. This is a common situation, especially among professional writers, in which one falls into a state of nonproduction, usually stemming from a lack of confidence in the quality of the work. It is especially common among people who have a reputation and are changing media (successful novelist turning screenwriter). We all have writer's block, to some degree, in that we all would benefit from writing more. We repress at least some of our writing because of uncertainty as to how it will be received. The same is true in other activities.

We are risk avoiders, and Freud would attribute this to our upbringing and its imprint upon our ego and superego. We are not gamblers unless the odds are sharply slanted in our favor (except for an occasional suicidal dash at the gaming tables).

Freudian theory leads us to expect conservatism and tells us that we must consciously argue with our egos and superegos if we are to deviate from our usually proven problem-solving vocabulary. This argument is not easy. Another Freudian concept is that of rationalization, in which we interpret our feelings in the most acceptable terms we can. If we fail to follow up a creative idea, we may convince ourselves that it would not have been accepted, or that we really did not want to spend the time to develop it, or whatever. If we do not take an opportunity to join an exciting business start-up we may convince ourselves that it would have destroyed our marriage or that the company is destined to fail. Rationalization allows us to not only avoid risk but also to convince ourselves that it was for the better.

However, Freudian theory also leads us directly to creativity techniques or at least tactical approaches to managing creativity. Freudians and neo-Freudians hypothesize that we would be more creative and better able to deal with change if we were less neurotic. An example of this viewpoint is found in the book *Neurotic Distortion of the Creative Process* by Lawrence Kubie, written in 1966. This book captures the spirit of many people working with creativity who feel that neuroses are the main enemy of creativity — that the mentally healthy human will be more creative. There is some controversy here, since there have been so many obviously gifted and creative people who did not seem to be paragons of psychological health. Critics of Kubie's viewpoint will point to examples like Van Gogh, who was obviously creative, but perhaps suffered from neuroses. The Freudians counter such examples nicely by hypothesizing that Van Gogh and his ilk would have been even more creative had they been less psychologically tortured.

For most of us, it is probably true that fewer neuroses mean greater creativity. However, directly addressing neuroses is not trivial. The best approach is therapy of some sort, and therapy is time-consuming, expensive, and somewhat unpredictable in its effects. If you or your family or organization are yearning for an increase in creativity, therapy is not the first option you should consider. It may be that your inability to finish your novel is becoming so painful that a therapist could help you. However, it is less likely that your group at work is going to visit a therapist and not likely at all that you are going to convince your entire company to enter therapy. Not only is therapy time-consuming, expensive, and unpredictable, but its focus on concerns of interpersonal behavior and personality tend to outweigh those such as intellectual problem solving.

How about more modest interventions — those that are not oriented toward personality change? Here, of course, we have a wealth of possibilities. There are myriad activities that relax the ego and the superego and let ideas that are on the margins of feasibility and practicality exist for a while. A playful and humorous environment will accomplish this, as will a psychological environment structured specifically to do so. Group brainstorming is a good example. Some creativity consultants employ activities like finger painting to "loosen people up."

LAUGHING AT OUR FEARS

Let's talk a bit in more detail about humor, since it is beneficial to creativity and change and easy to utilize. As we mentioned after the zoo exercise, humor first of all allows us to take risk. The animal sound is much easier to manufacture if our observer is capable of humor. It is a louder exercise in an informal group of friends or professional colleagues than in a formal gathering of strangers. We are much better at exposing our frailties if a mishap is received with gentle humor than cold judgment. As situations grow more serious, we naturally expect the chuckles to decrease in intensity. However, a form of humor remains available to help us take risks. In the extreme there is a humor, sometimes called "black" humor, which saves us. Probably at some time in your life you have been in a particularly grim situation from which you simply did not see how you were going to escape. You were saved because things kept getting worse until they finally appeared funny. At that point you were able to move. The same thing also happens to groups and organizations in a time of emergency. Although sometimes socially out of place, humor is more than helpful in times of crisis.

Humor not only allows us to take more risk, but also accompanies a decrease in tension. Jokes are based on this fact. A joke builds tension by stating a problem with an unknown solution, telling a story with an unknown ending, or merely through the commitment of the teller of the joke. The punch line drops this tension and our reaction is to laugh. Two examples are given here — a long one and a short one. As you read them, see if you can feel tension build and then drop at the punch line. If it does, you will laugh.

Joke #1

How do you tell the difference between a runover attorney (physician, teenager, etc.) and a runover snake?
There are skidmarks in front of the snake.

Joke #2

An elderly friend of mine used to drop into his favorite neighborhood bar late each Friday afternoon and have two drinks. He would then arrive home relaxed and spend the evening with his wife. These relaxed evenings together had become one of their favorite traditions. However, one Friday evening he did not return home until quite late and was obviously not well when he walked through the door. His wife, of course, was beside herself with worry but after a bit she realized that my friend was simply drunk. She helped him into bed and went to bed herself. The next day he awoke with a terrible hangover and was generally out of sorts until about noon. However, she did what she could for him and hid her disappointment concerning their missed evening. Finally, however, he felt better and she could no longer resist asking him what had happened. His story was:

On leaving his favorite bar he for the first time noticed a beautiful golden door in a building on the way to his home. The door was surmounted with a magnificent golden canopy and fitted with a large golden knob. He was so curious that he tried the knob and the door opened, admitting him to a magnificent bar in which everything was golden. The rug and drapes were golden, the tables and chairs were golden, the golden bar had a golden rail, and the bartenders wore golden uniforms. The glassware was golden and the mirrors had golden frames. And, he remarked, even the urinal was golden. He was so taken by the surroundings that he ordered a drink, then another, then several others, and by the time he had recovered from the splendor of the bar, he was quite drunk.

This story seemed believable to his wife, but she was bothered by the unusual nature of the description and by the fact that this bar should have suddenly appeared on a route used for so many years by her husband. In order to assure herself that he was not suffering from age-related disabilities, she decided to check his story. She did this by telephoning bars and asking the person who answered, "Does your bar have a golden door?" She called several bars and the answer was always a polite no. Finally she called a bar and the man who answered replied, "Why, yes, it does." She then proceeded to question him further. "Does your door have a golden canopy over it and a golden knob?" "Yes ma'am." "Does your bar have a golden rug and drapes?" "Yes." "Golden tables and chairs and a golden bar with a golden rail?" "Yes ma'am." "Do your bartenders have golden uniforms?" "Yes." "Do you have golden glassware and golden mirror frames?" "Yes." "Do you have a golden urinal?"

At this point she heard the man partially cover the phone, turn away, and say, "Hey, Ed, we got a line on the guy who pissed in the saxophone."

Did you follow the tension? It is a good rule to use to design your own joke. The phenomenon is important to us because solving a problem also releases tension. The feelings of Einstein mentioned in Chapter 4 accompanied a release of tension. In the midst of working on a long and serious problem we are not likely to suddenly burst out in laughter (unless the problem is too much for us). However, feelings of lightness, if not downright joy, accompany creative insights. We therefore assume that humor is a necessary ingredient of successful creativity and response to change, and, if it disappears, we are in trouble.

There are other creativity interventions that modify the ego and superego with less humor, of course. Some simply are based on rules that change the judgmental criteria. If I give a class a project and tell them the best grades will go to the most flaky results, I will (providing I can rigorously define flaky) receive material that would ordinarily never be produced by my students. We can also deal with emotions in an analytical way in regular life as well as in Freudian analysis. Considering emotion as a necessary part of the problem-solving process is extremely valuable in situations of creativity and change.

REWARD SYSTEM

We have discussed the nature of risk and the benefits of confronting it directly and handling it rationally. We have spoken about the emotions involved and the need to deal with them intelligently. What else can we do to handle the risk inherent in creativity and change? One of the most critical issues in managing creativity and change is the issue of reward systems.

Just as Freudian theory gave us some insight into the emotions involved with risk, so does the psychological theory of behaviorism tell us about the importance of reward systems. This theory dominated psychology from the early part of the twentieth century until recently and is associated with such names as J. B. Watson, E. P. Pavlov, E. L. Thorndike, and B. F. Skinner. If you took a psychology course in school it was probably heavily biased toward behaviorism, with its emphasis on stimulus and response and experiments performed with rats and pigeons.

At present there is somewhat of a reaction against behaviorism, probably due to its past success. However, it still helps us understand much human behavior, serves as the basis of a great amount of educational theory, and gives us a unique insight into human problem solving. Although behaviorists certainly neglect much of that which is uniquely human, it is the psychological theory that is most consistent with the emphasis on habit discussed in the earlier parts of this book.

Behaviorists believe that our behavior is determined by events in our past experience. We are born with unformed circuits and continually add details to our wiring through experience in our environment. Many of the experiments performed by the behaviorists have had to do with conditioning. They typically made use of reward and/ or punishment to change behavior in order to better understand how behavior is learned. In the many famous experiments of B. F. Skinner, for instance, the subjects were placed in an apparatus in which a reward was given if a problem was solved (rats pressed a lever for a pellet of food, pigeons pecked a disk for food). The subjects were allowed to remain in the box for a long period of time and their behavior was observed over this time. As in many conditioning experiments, the response to the stimulus strengthened with repetition. The rat became much more efficient at pushing the pedal after a number of successes. Also, if the reward was not presented, extinction of the learned response occurred. Original experiments were typically done with animals receiving a reward of something pleasant (food) or the avoidance of something unpleasant (electric shock). However, if another stimulus was paired with the primary reinforcer, it eventually provided secondary reinforcement for an act. In this way, for instance, chimpanzees could be taught first of all to insert tokens into a vending machine to receive food and then to operate another device that dispensed tokens.

The importance of behaviorism to us, of course, is that although most conditioning experiments have been done on so-called lower animals, conditioning also works very well indeed with us exalted humans. We are creatures of our past conditioning and respond disturbingly well to reward and punishment. Like Pavlov's dogs, who were conditioned to salivate at the sound of a buzzer, we often respond the way we would to a stimulus when we encounter another phenomenon. For instance, feelings we experienced in schools or in former jobs as a result of educational or professional activities are often evoked by a visit to the environment in which these activities occurred. Do you feel differently when you awaken on a working day rather than on a weekend? Why? Isn't it perhaps because you have been conditioned by the activities that usually occur on these two types of day? Do you feel different when you visit your family home? If you feel uncomfortable around mathematics or poetry or painting or science, try to figure out where these feelings come from. Conditioning is a reasonable explanation for them. Instead of dog food you may have been given a blow to your self-esteem. The natural response was to feel bad rather than salivate. The buzzer was a long division problem, or a self-appointed poetry or painting expert snubbing you, or a clumsy bout with high school chemistry. You have been conditioned to use certain problem-solving approaches such as the habits discussed in Chapter 4. The following exercise may help you to think about this.

EXERCISE

See how many examples you can think of in which conditioning has negatively influenced your problem-solving ability. A good place to start is to examine problem-solving situations that you avoid.

There is also good news, of course. According to the behaviorists, conditioning has made us what we are. It has resulted in our learning the skills, knowledge, and techniques that we use in solving the problems of life. You can do a positive version of the preceding exercise and think of a type of problem solving at which you are highly competent. If you then consider the role that conditioning has played, you will probably conclude that it has done you more good than harm.

How, then, do we get ourselves or others to do new things — to be more creative and better adapt to change? The behavioral psychologists would certainly prescribe reward and/or punishment. They would even go further, and suggest that if we use rewards to encourage people to be more creative, they will "learn" this behavior. Although we consider ourselves superior beings, we humans are no less fond of rewards. Hopefully we are better at consciously solving problems than Pavlov's dogs, Thorndike's cats, or Skinner's rats. If I, an engineer, am placed in a cage with an intricate latch mechanism and a reward outside of the door, I will probably first of all examine the latch and attempt to match my mental model of the mechanism with my knowledge and experience of mechanisms. If the components are all visible, it is even likely that my first physical move will be successful. However, the principles of conditioning still define what I do; they are just not as evident. I also, like the dog, cat, and rat, will go for the reward.

We hear more about behavior modification than problem-solving modification. It is important to realize that rewards, punishment, and repetition can change not only behavior but also attitudes and cognitive processes. Look at education as an example. In an experiment performed at Carnegie-Mellon University, tests of creativity and of analytical ability were given over a four-year time period to a random sample of art students and engineering students. The scores showed that a cognitive approach to problem solving can be affected by a system of reward, punishment, and exercise. The engineers, who were rewarded as students for extrapolating basic scientific principles to "right" answers, became stronger at analysis, which is the fundamental thought process involved. They became weaker at creativity, since engineering students have little chance to practice it in their course work and are, in fact, punished if they come up with a "creative" answer as to how thick a beam should be. The art students, on the other hand, became stronger in creativity and weaker in analytical ability as measured by the tests. This is consistent with the stress placed upon creative activities in art courses.

If we believe that we are risk adverse and that increasing creativity and change lead us into increased risk, we have to wonder why any rational person would opt for increased change and creativity? The answer must have to do with reward. There must be something in it for us: increased satisfaction, attainment of a goal, avoidance of dissatisfaction, or something else to compensate for the possible losses and the emotional state connected with leaving an equilibrium state for one with more unknowns. I am assuming, as I have throughout this book, that any individual, group, or organization is in an equilibrium state as far as creativity and change are concerned. If creativity and change are at such a low level that people are frustrated and bored, the reward is obvious. We all have an internal need for a certain level of creativity and change in our lives. If we are below this level we do not speak of rewards, we speak of escape. However, it is more often the case that we are reasonably challenged; change and creativity on the job balanced against that off of the job; dynamic activities balanced against static; unknowns balanced against knowns. In other words, life is pretty good. If creativity and change are to be increased in this type of situation, the reward system becomes overridingly important. There must be something in it for us to rock the boat — to take more risk.

Before we become more involved in the discussion of rewards, we should return a moment to the topic of intrinsic and extrinsic rewards. Experiments and folklore have indicated that we are more creative when intrinsically motivated and when we work in an atmosphere that is light on evaluation and judgment. What causes us to work hard in these situations? Our inherent interest in and fascination with the task. Our rewards consist of our own satisfaction with our achievements. What does this say to us? It says that if we can and do rearrange our schedule to spend more time on the things in which we are extremely interested, assuming that we have the time and support to keep the wolves away from our door, we will increase our creativity. It also says that groups and organizations should be more creative if the involved individuals are allowed to do the same. We should take special effort to match people to tasks that they will be motivated to do through interest rather than through external reward.

Why not always rely upon intrinsic rewards? Even if involved in activities that are so pleasurable that motivation is intrinsic, most of us have wolves. The people I know, for better or worse, are old friends with external motivation in life. I am a good example. In general I consider myself extremely fortunate in that I am involved in activities that bring great satisfaction to me. However, the activities that bring me pleasure are complex. I have not yet found a way to escape the short-term drudgery and trauma that accompany my long-term satisfaction. I am continually fighting against my schedule and the clock to finish activities that are not as much fun to me as alternates I can think of (my hobbies, reading trashy novels, daydreaming). I am often aware of my income and the opinions of others. I am affected by rewards and often evaluated. Am I weak? Should I tell the world to bug off, find a rich patron, and settle down to the things I most love to do in the short term? I don't think so. I am afraid that I would lose in the long run. I am afraid that I am normal. The things that give me long-term satisfaction require short-term agony. My values seem to vote against rich patrons. I live in a world of heavy extrinsic motivation. In this world, evaluation, inadequate resources, and peer opinion are part of life. Rewards must be designed and put into place to add to extrinsic motivation.

The next chapter will discuss the proper design of rewards.

10

Rewards — The Necessary Pot of Gold

If rewards are to be successful in stimulating creativity and response to change, they must meet a need. This is true whether we are rewarding ourselves or others. The humanistic psychologist Abraham Maslow developed the hierarchy of needs shown in Figure 10-1. According to Maslow, if the lower needs are not filled, we concentrate exclusively upon satisfying them. When our lower needs are filled to an acceptable level, we begin to put our energies into fulfilling our higher needs. For instance, if our physical needs are not satisfied, we concentrate on finding food, water, and whatever else we need to keep our body going. However, as soon as we have these needs somewhat satisfied (not totally sated), we become interested in the next level, which has to do with feeling safe. These two bottom levels have to do with our individual animal well-being in the present and in the future. After we have our safety needs somewhat fulfilled, we progress on to the levels having to do with the opinion of others. These needs can be satisfied only if we reach a position in our society where others welcome and respect us. Unlike the bottom two need levels in the figure, we may not be able to sate these needs. We can eat as much as we can hold but we may never have enough love or respect. The top three needs in Figure 10-1 have

FIGURE 10-1 Maslow's Hierarchy of Needs

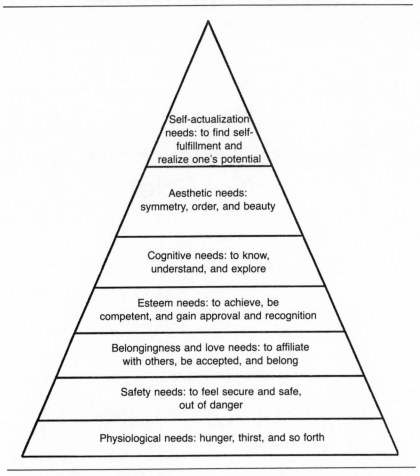

to do with thinking and problem solving. They are expressions of the individual and are directly pertinent to the subject of this book. We may also have difficulty in sating these needs, especially those of us blessed/cursed with a strong love of achievement.

Most people who read books like this have satisfied the bottom two levels of need in Figure 10-1 to a reasonable extent. Our bodies are provided for and safe. We have a paycheck and some security. What does the next level of social needs say to us as far as problem solving? They say that we want to belong to groups and affiliate with our peers. How can we most easily do this? Socialization necessarily places constraints upon us — do's and don'ts and required values.

The way one can most easily become accepted in a group is to adopt these; to act like the others in the group. Social acceptance can therefore come through conformity in problem solving as well as in action.

A widely referenced study from the realm of social psychology was performed by Solomon Asch. In this study experimental subjects were seated at a table with other subjects. The group was then shown two displays, one with a single line and one with three lines (see Figure 10-2). Each person in turn was asked to judge which of the three lines were the same length as the single line. The answer should have been obvious. However, all of the other subjects (actually paid shills) gave the same incorrect response. The response of the actual subject obviously depended upon where he or she was seated in the answering queue and, therefore, how many people had gone before. The subjects were so influenced by the others in the group that they would frequently give the wrong answer. Three-quarters of the subjects did this at least once. If just one of the shills gave the proper answer while the rest stuck with the wrong answer, this fraction dropped to 1/16th. However, in the face of united opposition, compliance was extraordinarily high. Our social needs tell us strongly to conform.

Although these conforming needs lead us toward conventional wisdom, converging meetings, and common social mores, they are

FIGURE 10-2 Asch's Lines

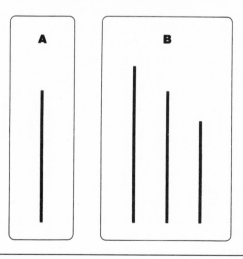

not always beneficial. In fact, if we are looking for deviance from the usual (creativity and change), they are counterproductive. They lead us to "group think." Remember the discussion about group intellect associated with Figure 6-2? Maslow's belonging needs push people toward commonality of habit. Many group creativity techniques attempt to change the group values so that belonging needs can be channeled toward the desired activity. In brainstorming, for instance (see Chapter 11), one is accepted by the group for cognitive outputs that might be considered rather extreme outside of the group.

What can we say about ego needs? First of all, they may pull us in opposite directions than the social needs in a group. Fulfilling ego needs requires influencing the group. The ego needs can cause us to seek dominance and therefore suppress the inputs of others. They also motivate us to achieve and to be competitive, two valuable components of problem solving. The professional world depends upon ego needs, at least in certain areas, for its well-being. A common method of satisfying both ego and belonging needs is to think of a creative idea and then attempt to drag the world with us. This is most convenient in an organization seeking increased creativity, since it results in implementation if successful. The desire to satisfy both belonging and ego needs is also one of the attractions of management. Presumably if we are good managers, we belong to an enterprise that values us and can influence others to follow us. The desire to satisfy both may also be part of the quest for junior high student office, rank in our fraternal organizations, and large numbers of pets.

The source of these ego needs is complex and their nature particularly human. Certainly the need to know, to understand, and to explore may have something to do with our animal origins. It is necessary to learn and to make our way in the world. However, what about the aesthetic need — the quest for symmetry, order, and beauty? This is vital to our well-being, but obviously operate far above the mere need to stay alive. Finally, how about the self-actualization need — the push to discover what we can be? These higher needs obviously have a great deal to do with sophisticated problem solving and we will have more to say about them later.

The hierarchy of needs in Figure 10-1 obviously has a great deal to do with reward systems. In order to be effective, rewards must be applied to needs that are operational. If I am successful in life and gaining weight, food will not be as important to me as if I am subsisting on a starvation diet. I have tenure in a university and would have to be quite colorful indeed to be dislodged. I am therefore not as tempted by offers of increased occupational safety as friends of mine in more volatile occupations. If I had no income, a large family, and huge financial obligations, you might be able to get me to face large amounts of uncertainty and risk through my physical and safety needs. However, if you are trying to encourage me to do so in my present state, you had better aim for my belonging and ego needs.

You may wonder how monetary rewards enter into the need framework. For those facing shortages of the necessities of life, money can obviously be used to help satisfy physical and safety needs. However, for those who have the good fortune to have these basic needs somewhat satisfied, money allows satisfaction of belonging and ego needs. It would be crass to suggest that money can buy acceptance, respect, satisfaction, and love, but money can be used to subsidize the search. Money is flexible in that it can be oriented toward satisfying our operational needs.

CREATIVITY FOR CASH

Remember the poem/drawing/math problem exercise? If it was uncomfortable, it was because you were taking risk. Supposing I offered you $500 to do this exercise? Would your attitude be different? Why? There are two reasons why such motivation might be effective here. First of all, you are used to taking risk for a reward. You might simply decide this is a worthwhile deal. Second, the money dignifies the loss (if any). If someone is willing to pay that much money for doing this simple task, you expect that there will be some discomfort in it. Therefore, you do not consider the discomfort as something to be avoided. In addition, you probably consider the task to be important.

Money is one of the more commonly used rewards in our culture. We are not at all surprised if those who are obviously involved in risky pursuits receive sizable financial rewards if they are successful. The entrepreneur starting an electronics company is expected to become wealthy if he or she succeeds. No one minds the retired astronaut gaining economic rewards from appearances in advertisements. We even extend this reasoning to groups and organizations. Many people I know cheered Chrysler's comfortable profits after they came back from oblivion. However, we are less liable to extend this same thinking to "normal" individuals, groups, and organizations that are at some time asked to take more risk. I am reminded of a maddening period I spent on the educational committee of a company I once worked for. The company was quite interested in continuing education for its effect on creativity and wanted its engineers to gain advanced degrees through part-time study. Part-time study while one is working and raising a family is not always fun, but the engineers did, in fact, take courses and slowly gain their degrees. However, when they finally received their degrees, no reward would follow. It was quite often the case that they would not gain a salary increment equal to that attached to the advanced degree in the case of an outside hire. Many of them finally realized that in order for their paycheck to reflect their degree they had to quit, go to work for another company, and then be hired back by our company. The company was just not willing to offer its own employees the same monetary reward they would give to those coming in from outside. The same is often true of risk.

Is money effective in promoting change and creativity? Ask yourself whether you would take more risk if there were a fat monetary reward awaiting. If you work in a profit-making company consider the following hypothetical situation:

> You are involved in a project that will hopefully make money for the company. The president (the chairman, if you are the president) calls you and explains the importance of the project. Furthermore, says the president, the company realizes that there is risk involved in this project, since a large amount of scarce capital will necessarily be invested in it and the company's position is such that if it fails there will not be time or money for a second attempt. The company is, if you would, betting itself on the new project. You are then given a choice. You can remain on your present career path (you are doing well) or you can be frozen in your present position and at your present salary (plus cost of living increases) until the project is over (say, _____ years) at which point you will receive _____ percent of the profit from the project. (Fill in appropriate numbers.)

Which deal would you choose? Would you act differently under the two reward systems?

A large number of people would like a financial reward that is more directly proportional to their creativity. Much to my amazement, a few years ago freshmen began arriving at college interested in a life that would give them equity. Whether they had vicariously lost faith in paychecks and retirement plans through the inflation of the late 1970s and early 1980s or whether this was merely part of the new entrepreneurial psychology, I do not know. Certainly in the area in which I live (culturally influenced by the famous Silicon Valley), there are a large number of people who would like to be "kept" entrepreneurs. They do not want to quit their jobs and put their entire life into starting a company, either because they are not interested in the game or because they do not want to put the requisite effort into the activity. However, they would like to move in that direction and would do so if rewarded in some manner that guaranteed the tuition payments and the mortgage and made the remainder of their income proportional to the success of their work.

It is not unusual for successful entrepreneurs to end up as spokespeople for the companies they founded. When the companies become large and if they run into an economic squeeze, the entrepreneurs often will bemoan what to them appears to be an inadequate level of creativity and innovation in the companies. If the level of creativity is inadequate, the problem can be looked at from the viewpoint of the reward system. When companies begin, the founders are usually highly creative. In fact, when companies are small, the environment is optimal for creativity. What is the motivation for this creativity? What is the reward for successful creativity on the part of the founders? I think we can agree that although a good deal of it is success in growing a company, money is in the background. When companies are large, the environment is no longer always optimal for creativity. We will talk about this much more in Chapter 11. The top management is no longer doing the nuts-and-bolts innovation. In the case of a technology-based company, it is done by the engineers. I have worked as an engineer in large technology-based companies and I know what is involved in innovation. It is not easy. One often becomes extraordinarily visible in doing such things because it becomes necessary to beg resources from all of one's friends. The results of a failure are measurable. The local world knows you have used up scarce resources and nothing has resulted. The results of a success are also measurable. One's technical reputation rises, one becomes more visible to top management, and one is more assured of similar tasks in the future. However, the effect upon one's paycheck is small. If one simply does a "good" job instead of a highly creative job, the financial reward is about the same and one's stomach and spare time remain intact. The potential economic reward for founding entrepreneurs is extraordinarily large compared to that available to the people expected to innovate within large companies. It is clear that if the monetary reward for creativity and change were increased, that the activities themselves might follow.

Why, then, isn't money more commonly used as a reward for creativity and change? As individuals we do not think in terms of giving ourselves money for success. We could. It would be easy to promise myself cash to spend foolishly upon completion of this book and it would probably make me move faster. However, I haven't. Some things we do may win us money. However, many creative things we do in our individual lives do not lead directly to cash. We have the option of embarking on ventures that may make us money (such as starting a company), but most of us do not choose to do so.

How about in our working lives? In addition to the intrinsic/extrinsic motivation argument, there are four main reasons why money is not used more often as a direct reward. First of all, it is money. It seems cheaper for an organization to pay on a salary basis for services delivered than on a basis that is proportional to the impact of a creative idea. There comes a time in the history of most companies in which those in charge may even become annoyed at the value of the equity owned by the founders. Second, companies like reward structures that are consistent with the rank of their employees. It is inconvenient to have an engineer taking home more money per year than the president. Rewards specifically for creative accomplishment also seem to be inconsistent with the team concept that is so prevalent in management. Most organizations are leery about giving an individual credit or even credit to a specific group. It is much easier to act as though the effort is a result of the efforts of the entire organization. Then one does not have to worry about jealousies and feelings of inequity. Finally, monetary rewards can complicate life for managers. I gave a talk a year or so ago to a company interested in increasing creativity. I recently heard from one of its managers that they had returned home from their retreat and tried an experiment. A particular software design team of eight people was beginning work on a project that the managers assumed would take a year. They asked the team to estimate the earliest date the project could be completed if all went well and if people worked as hard as they could. The answer came back as eight months. This was a project that would result in a large profit if it was finished earlier, so the company offered the team a cash reward of $80,000 ($10,000 per person) if they completed the project in eight months. So far, so good, right? They were one week late! What would you have done as manager of the team? This is one of those situations where there is no good answer. The company gave each member of the group $100. I imagine this makes you groan. However, any solution to the problem would result in some groaning.

These arguments are all valid. The counterargument is that monetary rewards offset the risks involved in creativity and change. There is an increasing amount of experimentation taking place at present. As an example from business, the commission is reemerging in sales. In the past there was a swing toward providing salaries in marketing, not only because it appeared more "professional," but also because sales forces accept corporate goals more easily if they involve selling products that are extremely difficult to move. However, recently people have rediscovered the motivating force of the commission. If you sold one hundred widgets last year and made $50,000 and, if next year I pay you $25,000 and $250 per widget, how many will you sell? The answer is probably more than one hundred. In order to sell more than one hundred you just may become more creative and change your ways. It is not unusual to offer cash rewards to hourly employees for creative suggestions. In fact, these awards are often a direct function of profit or savings (for example, 10 percent of the net savings over the next year). However, in the recent past, it has been unusual to see cash awards being given to salaried people. However, there is now an increase in rewards to salaried people for creative achievements of the type that would be expected of them anyway.

There are also examples of effective indirect uses of monetary reward in promoting creativity and change. In many of these, new activities lead to rapid advancement in a traditional hierarchy, one of the benefits being economic. In one large company that has long had such a system, an employee or a group of employees can present a product concept to a corporate evaluation board. If they find that it has good market potential and is compatible with their business, they will capitalize the development of the concept. If capable, the employee or group supervisor may remain head of the project, which, if successful, will become a division of the company. The project manager will then reap the rewards of a fast organizational climb. This policy was installed because the company has long had a philosophy that at least 25 percent of their sales should be based on products that did not exist five years previously. The policy has worked magnificently. In fact, one of this company's major present worries is its overabundance of divisions, which makes for a rather complex organization chart. Such a reward system, of course, gives the winner much more than money. The psychological rewards associated with promotion and peer esteem are also gained.

PSYCHOLOGICAL REWARDS

Psychological rewards are not as controversial as money. We do not have to worry about capital flow and salary equity, *and* they are very effective. There are fears about the use of these rewards (they should not be necessary, they will destroy the team, etc.). However, I have rarely observed serious harm caused by well-thought-out psychological rewards. It is true that in certain cases colleagues of a person receiving an individual award will feel more deserving than the recipient. However, there seems to be enough pragmatism/cynicism in all of us to weather that storm and, on the positive side, we realize that someone cares (they just gave the reward to the wrong person). Similarly, in most healthy situations, people are quite pleased when one or a few among them come into possession of something nice. Finally, I have seen few situations where rewards were overdone, especially psychological ones. It is theoretically possible, but most of us are so biased in the other direction that it is not a real worry.

The proper design of psychological rewards is a subtle process. Psychological rewards can take many forms and, once again, we are talking about both internal and external rewards. One of the benefits of psychological rewards is that external ones can be internalized. This process is worth some thought. The person who is consistently rewarded for a good chase independently of the kill will come to consider himself or herself a better chaser and, in turn, gain more pleasure from it independent of whether a kill is made or not. The employee who profits from a win in a situation involving creativity and change will be more likely to seek similar situations in the future and be more comfortable in them. Successes build confidence and nonterminal failures lessen the fear of failure. People who are well rewarded for creative acts can become self-styled "idea people," obsessed by the need for originality and crusading for others to recognize the "truth."

This internalization of reward can be all to the good should a permanent increase in creativity and change be desired. However, it can have certain costs. First of all, many people and organizations want to increase the level of creativity just until a problem is solved, not permanently. The same is true of change. Automobile companies in the United States found it necessary to accommodate to changes in consumer values and overseas competitive patterns in the early 1980s, but they are not necessarily eager to live this way in the future. Once the rewards consistent with increased creativity and change are internalized, it is difficult to reverse the process. The glory of inventing a new approach to assembling cars may outshine the routine of supervising an assembly line in steady-state operation. The wonder of writing poems for our neighborhood paper may cause the lawn to grow long indeed.

Research and experience has indicated other criteria for the design of successful psychological rewards for creativity and change. They should first of all be applied directly to those doing outstanding work with the maximum possible fanfare. Experiments performed by social psychologists (to be discussed in the next chapter) on "getting involved" indicate that individual recognition causes people to be more productive in a situation of creativity and change than if they are allowed to be anonymous in the group. They also imply that we should be particularly careful that people realize the key character of their roles. Social psychologists agree with the humanistic psychologists that creativity and change are supported by situations in which one can simultaneously be accepted by a group and be personally rewarded for the desired activities.

Experiments also indicate that rewards should be recognition for unusual achievement rather than for output that could be considered to be business as usual. Not surprisingly, rewards that make us feel good about our creativity accomplish more toward increasing creativity than simply being paid for our labor. Successful founders of companies enjoy their wealth. However, I believe that they enjoy it as a symbol of their creative ability as much as for what it can buy. Recognition for our cleverness is always welcome and reinforces our motivation to be creative. Reward for a good chase, even though we may not make the kill, is unexpected and delightful. Reward for successful accomplishment is more expected and, although valuable, is not as effective in increasing the creativity content of our self-images.

LEVELS OF THE GAME

One of the difficulties faced by those who manage others is to select rewards that fit others, instead of themselves. The perspectives of the various schools of psychology are particularly valuable in this respect. They cause us to put conscious effort into choosing the proper pot of gold to give to people. Otherwise our programmed mind confuses the purpose of the reward by applying our own set of values.

As an example, it is helpful to consider the stage of life that people are in when determining rewards. Most studies of stages have been done by developmental psychologists, who traditionally have worried about children. However, there have been exceptions. Table 10-1 shows a model of psychological stages developed by a psychologist named Erik Erikson. Unfortunately, this model is extraordinarily general and is based on the recognition of overall swings in life rather than detailed research into the human condition. It is a glorious oversimplification of the race we run.

Strangely enough, researchers are only now beginning to seriously study adult developmental psychology. Phrases such as "midlife crisis" and "male menopause" have been used only recently. In fact, much of the recent popular debate on psychological stages of life has occurred since the publication of Gail Sheehy's popular book *Passages*. This book is a description of stages that we go through. It is, of course, a very general statement, since we do not all go through these stages in order and on time. It is also somewhat extreme, as best-selling books are likely to be. However, it is of importance in our society because it caused the general public to begin to wonder about motivations that might be related to age.

TABLE 10-1 Erikson's Eight Stages of Man

Approximate age	Developmental task of that stage	Psychosocial crisis of that stage
0–1½ years	Attachment to mother, which lays foundations for later trust in others	Trust versus mistrust
1½–3 years	Gaining some basic control of self and environment (e.g., toilet training, exploration)	Autonomy versus shame and doubt
3–6 years	Becoming purposeful and directive	Initiative versus guilt
6 years–puberty	Developing social, physical, and school skills	Competence versus inferiority
Adolescence	Making transition from childhood to adulthood; developing a sense of identity	Identity versus role confusion
Early adulthood	Establishing intimate bonds of love and friendship	Intimacy versus isolation
Middle age	Fulfilling life goals that involve family, career, and society; developing concerns that embrace future generations	Productivity versus stagnation
Later years	Looking back over one's life and accepting its meaning	Integrity versus despair

It is obvious that psychological stages of life, to the extent that they exist, influence our problem solving. We may be less likely to make major professional and economic commitments during our freewheeling 20s than our achieving 30s. We may be less likely to panic in our 60s over details that would have given us lower back problems in our 40s. Where do these stages come from? They are formed partially by our changing philosophies and value systems as we age. They are also formed partly by our society, which expects certain things from us at certain ages.

Psychological stages of life obviously have a great deal to do with the considerations we were discussing in the last chapter. Our egos and superegos change and, therefore, different inputs are needed to encourage us to play with concepts outside of our usual limits. Economic and psychological rewards are most effective if they match our needs and desires at different stages of life. Our egos may be easier to relax when we are fifteen than when we are sixty. Our superegos may behave in the reverse. A cash reward of $250 may be a bigger deal when we are twenty than when we are sixty. An honorary degree may mean more when we are middle-aged than adolescent.

"THIS YEAR'S AWARD GOES TO . . ."

Psychological rewards, as we have said, are very important in the management of creativity and change. There is increased recognition of the importance of these rewards today, but it has been slow in coming because it is in contradiction to some of our professed sophisticated social values. I have a quasi-serious theory that one of the moving forces in this direction has been the emergence of organized athletics for children. Many of us have children in organized sports, and many of these children win trophies and ribbons at an alarming rate. My children have shelves full of trophies and walls full of ribbons. I never won trophies and ribbons when I was a child. In fact, my children have more trophies and ribbons than I will ever win. This has given me an opportunity to see, through my jealousy, that I am undertrophied in life. I am not of an age, social status, or value system that lets me complain about this. However, I suspect that if it is true of me, it is true of a lot of other people. When I do occasionally get a trophy, my skill at rationalization lets me get rid of any clash with my professed social values instantaneously.

Let us dwell a bit more on trophies — cups, ribbons, medals, certificates, and the classic 1930s brass woman standing in front of simulated walnut on a plastic marble slab and holding a wreath aloft. I am always amused at the reaction of educated, sophisticated people to such things. I recently gave a talk on quality to a group of electronics company executives. I was talking about an aspect of quality that particularly interests me. This is the perceived value of quality — that which causes people to be willing to pay more for something than it is worth if measured by function alone. It is pertinent to our choice of cameras, computers, and automobiles if we happen to have a bit of extra disposable income. It is obviously important. However, the other speaker was talking on the type of quality associated with zero defects. Since I was sitting at the head table, I was able to both listen to him and watch the audience. He was giving a slide talk and his slides consisted of a mixture of philosophy, data, and pictures of quality groups. The pictures would typically show a number of people standing in front of a huge wall chart that was obviously a plot of defects over time, since it was decreasing toward zero. The people were wearing blazers that were inscribed with their names, the company logo, and something like "Quality Ace." In front of them was a huge trophy, replete with eagles, angels, wreaths, and other such things. They all looked very happy. I could tell by their whispering and nudging that the audience was having trouble with the pictures. In a sense, blazers, trophies, and names such as "Quality Ace" seemed a bit tacky for the professional high-technology semiconductor scene. However, these rewards seemed to be effective in accomplishing change and motivating creativity.

I have been involved in sales awards banquets for companies that sold consumer products. To managers of companies based on sophisticated technology, the amount of hype in these events is almost embarrassing. However, they are effective. People do like their trophies, even if they happen to be for "cutest" salesperson. I have also given many talks at events honoring employees who have accomplished something unusual (unusually large number of patent disclosures, accepted suggestions, etc). Typically they include a lunch in the company dining room, a talk by someone like me, a talk by a company executive, and the presentation of medals. One could not live very long on the proceeds from selling one of these medals. However, despite the flip comments during the session, my impression is that they are deeply appreciated.

PUBLICITY AND VISIBILITY

There are psychological rewards above and beyond trophies, of course. Professional visibility is one of the more important ones. It is a clever company that recognizes its employees for extraordinary achievement not only within the company but also outside of it. There is a perceived risk from outside visibility because of the possibility of pirating. However, the risk is more than offset by the reward to the employee. This visibility is standard procedure among faculty members in universities, since it is the basis for intellectual communication and advertising. It involves the presentation of papers, publication, and use of the media. It is an easy perquisite to offer to employees and pays great dividends. Particularly creative research and development groups are masters of this. Another good type of psychological award is plain old publicity, whether it be widespread or merely local. Writeups in company papers and displays of well-done jobs recognize employee contributions. Managerial compliments are perhaps the cheapest form of psychological feedback for good work. These can be either verbal or written and are extraordinarily valuable.

Why is psychological reward for risk-taking in situations involving high levels of creativity and change so rare if it is so cheap and effective? The reasons given previously having to do with conflict with professed social values are part of the problem. However, there are two more reasons. The first is that professional life is a life characterized by formalized personal interactions. Any baring of the soul is usually done as an adjunct to work, not as a part of it. It is all right to discuss family problems with your co-worker, but you probably do not do so with your boss or the janitor. In addition, many managers and supervisors simply have difficulty giving compliments. Either shyness or personal values get in the way. It is possible to manage business as usual with a minimum of psychological rewards (although it is dumb). However, in situations of increased risk, psychological reward is a management tool worthy of serious consideration.

REWARD FOR THE PROCESS

Another difficulty in giving rewards for professional creative achievement is that so many projects have no definite completion date. They evolve from problem statement through concept through detailing through fabrication and sales and into repair. Those involved cannot on a particular day say, "We are done." In fact, key people on a project sometimes slide from phase to phase and never feel that they are finished. There are, therefore, few points in time when rewards can be given. However, it is important to remember that we are talking about increased creativity and change here. In such situations we are in an experimental mode and can expect failures. In order to keep people motivated, we cannot reward entirely on successful completions. We must also reward the process if it is a good one. The juggling of reward for process and reward for output is an important task for a good manager of creativity and change. We are trying to keep high standards by being critical and tough-minded. However, we also have to reward the attempt, because we are asking people to involve themselves in a situation where there is no certainty that the endpoint will turn out to be consistent with the traditional grading system. It is, therefore, important to ensure that psychological rewards are given for heroic efforts as well as for exceptional products and that they are spread over time rather than being saved for a nonexistent finish date. Rewards are plentiful in well-managed organizations where creativity and change are at a high level.

These comments are equally valid for the individual managing his or her own creativity and change. Whether we are playing for a large future gain in material things or working for self-satisfaction, we will do better if we ensure that the end reward is there and that we receive reinforcement for our efforts along the way. This is particularly true because, as we mentioned earlier, we tend to underestimate the value of our own output. We need feedback. We also need to ensure that our rewards fit our needs, are consistent with our social situation, and are sensitive to our stage in life. We can be just as smart in designing reward systems for ourselves as for others.

Are you trying to complete some creative project such as a book in your spare time? You are probably not devoting enough time to it and not gathering enough input from other people. You must have some sort of expensive minor vice. Straight malt Scotch? A used Corvette? A trip? Figure out a scheme whereby you award yourself various installments of your vice upon completion of various creative milestones (chapter finished, approval by your most feared critic). You will be embarrassed to watch your creative output increase markedly through the application of such a tacky scheme. You may be forced to admit that you are human.

We have been discussing rewards that accompany a win. We would also like psychological protection against a loss. We live more easily with increased risk if we feel that a failure will not bring unacceptable loss to our psychological well-being. Most of us need to think of ourselves as winners. If we are asked to take on a risky task, we want protection. This protection can best take the form of understanding on the part of our superiors, our peers, and our subordinates as to the importance and riskiness of the task. This protection is critical because of our perception of the penalties that result from a loss.

Finally, since we so strongly need to belong, we want to feel that this risky life we are being asked to adopt is the best way to fly. We want to know that the respected and important life-style involves risk and failure. This is true whether we speak of individual values, group style, or corporate culture. Most creative organizational units I know spend considerable effort in reminding themselves of the generally admirable nature of a life filled with creativity and lightning-like response to change. This effort typically goes not only into establishing reward mechanisms such as those previously discussed but also into ensuring that the rewards and other reminders of the exemplary nature of creativity are well publicized. Creative companies and ones that can change easily have established cultures where it is obvious to everyone that not only is it "good" to live in such a way but also that the company appreciates it and treats well those who do it.

TWO MODEST PROPOSALS

We can also encourage creativity and change with interventions that change expectations and priorities. *If you want to become more creative as an individual, start spending more time with creative people.* Change your local culture to one that is more creative and change-oriented and your belonging needs will push you gently in that direction. Identification with those about you will cause you to try new things and think of yourself as more creative. You will then seek even more creative friends. See how easy it is? This approach is also easily used in groups and organizations. Typical components of a campaign to increase creativity and adaptability to change might include pertinent individual and group psychological and economic rewards as well as well-publicized company seminars and meetings featuring outstandingly creative people as guests. Employees can be encouraged to mingle with highly creative people within the organization and managers can spend more time with managers from highly creative enterprises. As a large-scale example of this, look at the turnaround in the attitude of US industry toward creativity in the last ten years. It was not a topic of great interest in 1976. However, because of national need, a great amount of hoopla, and a tremendous amount of activity, it is now on everyone's mind. The result cannot help but be increased creativity at all levels.

Another technique that receives too little attention is *plain old-fashioned cheerleading*. This is more subtle than merely rewarding success. Good cheerleaders, it is true, create a loud recognition of success. If a first down is made, they lead the crowd in noisy approval. However, good cheerleaders are supposed to keep going during periods of despondency and at the bottom end of a 56–0 score. In situations of creativity and change, cheerleading is beneficial, especially for less experienced people, who are often involved in situations in which they do not have the experience to know whether they are going to win or lose. They will look to management, and management is well advised to give them continual signals that they will win (even if management is not too sure). Professional cheerleading is not as vocal as cheerleading at football games. Some of the best professional cheerleaders are merely quietly confident and infectiously optimistic. Others use a style similar to that of a marine sergeant in combat. However, whatever the style, cheerleading is an essential ingredient in motivating and coordinating people in a creative and changing environment.

Let us now turn to considerations of organizational and management style. These are obviously of interest in situations where creativity and change involve numbers of people. However, there are implications concerning individual creativity that make the material of interest to everyone. Besides, as I said in the beginning, few of us implement anything without the help of others.

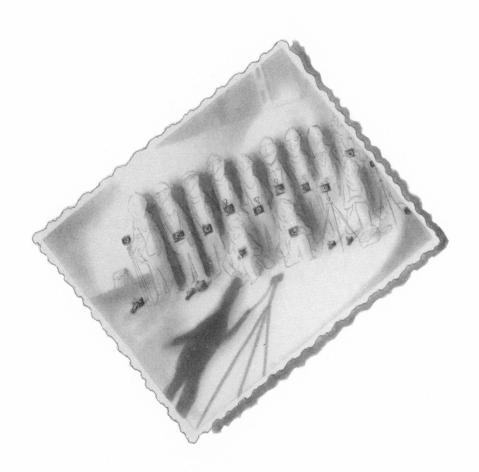

11

Pulling Together — Organizing for Creativity

The characteristics of organizations and groups play a very important role in the level of creativity and the ability to respond to change. It is folklore that small and flexible organizations managed in a participatory way are more capable of creativity and change. Before we go on to examine creativity in groups, it is worth exploring the advantages and disadvantages of size in order to see what lessons we can learn.

Large formal organizations have many advantages. One might suspect that this is true because small, flexible organizations seem always to strive to become larger, even though increased formalization is unavoidable. What is so attractive about size? First of all, large organizations make large impacts upon the world. Large businesses interact with large numbers of customers, make large amounts of money, and can have significant influence upon social institutions, governments, and individuals. Large universities can offer many programs and projects and focus sufficient resources to attain high quality. Large armies can overwhelm smaller ones, and large think tanks and architecture firms can often win contracts that smaller ones can't.

In a similar vein, large organizations can take on ambitious projects. I recently invited a retired engineering executive from McDonell Douglas Corporation to be a guest speaker in one of my classes. Many students are leary of the large-scale working environments of aircraft companies, and one of them asked my guest whether he would not have rather spent his career in a small company. His answer was simple — "Small companies can't make DC-10s." There is tremendous satisfaction in being involved in large-scale complex projects that involve a tremendous array of sophistication and interaction. One has only to spend time with someone involved in the design and construction of a large dam, ship, bridge, transportation system, or missile system to discover this. I was involved in the early days of the US space effort and you do not want to ask me about it unless you have quite a bit of free time. It was large and I loved it.

Large corporations are also stable. One of the first modern organizational theorists, a German sociologist named Max Weber, coined the word *bureaucracy*. To him this was a word with very positive connotations. A bureaucracy was a wonderful, stable structure. Large, formal organizations in which jobs are tightly defined and control is rigorously exerted according to lines of hierarchy are relatively insensitive to the loss (or gain) of individuals. This, we must admit, is an advantage, albeit one that sounds somewhat inhuman and that we tend to take for granted.

Large, formal organizations are also relatively stable in the face of changes in the market. They tend to have a wider diversity in products and customers that protects them against changes in demand for a single product or by a single customer group. Large organizations are also relatively stable during economic shifts. They tend to have access to large amounts of capital and are able to exert political force when necessary (witness the famous government loan to Chrysler).

Large corporations also offer certain advantages to employees. They offer predictable paychecks and a high degree of job stability. This is once again taken for granted by many people. However, it is impressive to those who have been without regular paychecks. I found at one time in my career, when I was involved in hiring, that it was surprisingly easy to hire consultants into salaried positions. The freedom and glamour of a free-lance existence often does not offset the wonder of a reliable paycheck. Large organizations also allow employees room to move and advance. It is possible to grow in one's career without sacrificing the specific knowledge one has obtained. In a similar fashion, large corporations provide a wide variety of mentors and opportunities to learn.

There are also advantages to managers in large corporations. First of all, they too have stability, regular pay, mentorship, and room to grow. There is also prestige (people at parties are more impressed by the president of General Motors Corporation than the president of the consulting company that consists of me and my wife). There are relatively large amounts of resources and opportunities to identify with the large social effects mentioned earlier.

Finally, growth itself is an advantage because it gives individuals more opportunity to increase the scale of their own operation and advance within a group or organization, lends excitement and a feeling of winning, and produces support from our growth-oriented culture. Have you been a member of an organization that voluntarily decided not to grow? They are rare, since most organizations can convince themselves that they could perform their work a bit better with a little more help. Even if the decision is made, no-growth is difficult to maintain because of its cost in morale. The university at which I work decided some time ago to not increase the size of the student body. This was a rational decision, because across the bay from this university is a very strong very large competitor that happens to receive a large stipend from the state of California. We must be clever in competing with this university. If we try to duplicate it, we will fail, since lack of subsidy will cause us to market a similar product at a much higher cost. Our advantage lies in being smaller, swifter, and friendlier to our high-paying students. However, even though our student population is fixed (almost) and our faculty size is somewhat fixed, we continue to grow in facilities, outside-funded activities, nonteaching staff, numbers of transactions per month, acres of lawn and parking, and myriad activities. Growth brings improved capability and room for individuals to move. It also soothes the empire-builder dwelling within most of us.

THE PATTERN OF GROWTH

If growth and resulting bigness have all of these positive attributes, why are the advantages of smallness so much in the limelight these days? After all, most large companies were at one time small. They have grown for valid reasons. However, they have not grown without costs, and these costs have to do with our topic of creativity and change. Figure 11-1 is from an article written by organizational behavior expert Larry Greiner. It details a process that will probably be familiar to you if you are or have ever been involved in any sort of

FIGURE 11-1 The Five Phases of a Corporation's Growth

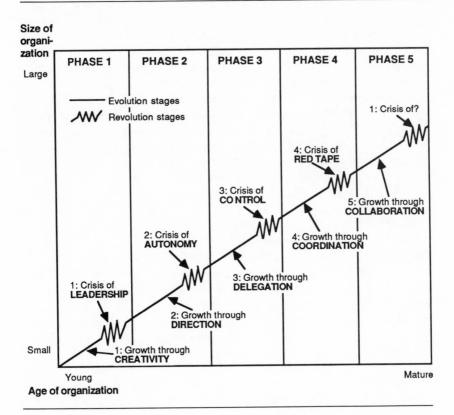

organization. The figure is a qualitative plot of growth over time. By its upward slope it implies that successful organizations will grow.

The figure describes phases of growth in an organization and illuminates crises that the author feels are common. These crises occur at the ends of stable phases and may be abrupt or lengthy. They may or may not cause displacements in management and over-all employment. Let us examine them and think about what they have to do with creativity and ability to respond to change.

The first phase on the curve represents the start-up. During this period the fledgling organization has a few to dozens of people, probably a unique product or service, very high motivation, pride of ownership and excitement among the employees, and informal and free communications. In the electronic business, this represents the revered "garage shop." Greiner calls it the creative phase because such an enterprise is capable of a high degree of day-to-day creativity.

Constraints are few and precedent is lacking. The people involved are proud of the fact that they are blazing new paths and must be clever to survive. If a problem arises, they solve it, because they have no choice.

The first crisis (leadership) occurs when the organization becomes large enough (perhaps on the order of one hundred people) that it can no longer operate efficiently through completely informal organizational methods. It has hired many employees that do not have a sense of ownership, it is tying up too much of its resources in inventory, jobs are overlapping and difficult to describe to new employees, enough people are around that criticism meets most moves, and the enterprise is being heavily influenced by the IRS and various attorneys. At this stage, the founders of the company, even though they can read the handwriting on the wall, seem not to be reacting rapidly enough. In certain dire cases, they may not even want to read the handwriting on the wall. It is not unusual for management to resist increased formalization to the point where higher powers influence them or at least augment them with other individuals who are more formal in their organizational philosophy. If the organization is to continue to be successful, it will adapt. It will adopt a greater degree of control and formality.

Organizational charts, job descriptions, clear hierarchies, inventory control and accounting systems, production control systems, and other such accoutrements will appear. This is not to say that the organizations must take on the philosophies of the nineteenth-century British Marine Corps. Management may remain approachable and informal in style and should preserve as much of the motivation of the start-up as possible, but it must somehow simplify life for the members of what is becoming a mob. Some organizations have such dislike of the trappings of traditional large organizations that they choose to exert control through nontraditional means (corporate belief systems, pseudo family authority structures). However, with growth, more control becomes necessary. Control and communication systems become formalized in order to ensure that effort is not consumed in redundancy and contradictory decisions. The people-oriented chief may continue to leave the door open to all employees. However, a lower percentage of people walk through it.

The organization now does very well indeed with its new control-oriented habits and continues its growth. It may continue to think of itself as a "small" company even as it grows and acquires competition. However, eventually it runs into trouble again. It becomes increasingly cumbersome, because as size increases, the advantages of a strict linear hierarchy tend to be overcome by the complexity of its own communication and control procedures. People at the working level must simply wait too long for permission to act from the top. A point is reached where delegation is necessary. Decisions must be made lower in the organization and such organizational entities as profit centers, product-based groups, and geographically decentralized operating units must be established. Once again, Mr. Greiner predicts a crisis. Managers may not be eager for a change and may be pushed from above. Managers who direct an organization during the "direction" phase may prefer a life that appears tidy to them. However, if the organization is to remain healthy, a change will occur and the organization will enter the "delegation" phase.

There are other stages and other crises on the curve. The next crisis occurs at the point when the divisions of the organization have become so strong that upper management realizes that they could become independent units. The organization will then usually respond by taking advantage of possible synthesis. Companies will become concerned with coordination, company image, product balance, centralized policy, logos, product identity, and so on. The next crisis occurs when the organization has become so large that it is floundering in red tape, litigation, political forces, and general complexity. Those interested in more details should read the article. For our purposes here, we must only decide whether we think that there is truth in the article (I obviously think that it is of almost biblical stature) and, if so, what it has to do with creativity and change.

As the folklore suggests, creativity and responsiveness to change are more natural in small organizations than large formal ones. In the start-up, probably no one is even thinking specifically about creativity and change. The organization just does it, without self-consciousness. Its problem-solving habits include creativity and a high rate of change. However, as it grows, it becomes necessary to become more self-conscious and to adjust the organization to provide the environment for the desired creativity and responsiveness to change. In business, it is not uncommon for a start-up to be dominated by people who are oriented toward the development of a product or service. As the organization grows, emphasis necessarily shifts toward manufacturing the product more efficiently and selling it, since as competition enters, selling becomes more difficult and costs become a significant concern. At this point, the development of follow-up products and services often receives short shrift. At some point it becomes necessary to provide consciously for these activities. As organizational rewards shift toward those who control and cut costs, it is necessary to ensure that rewards for the development of new products and services do not stop. As resources move from product development to marketing to manufacturing, it is necessary to make sure that resources remain in product development and marketing. At a later phase, as delegation occurs, it becomes necessary to worry about whether time, effort, and rewards are made available to encourage creativity and response to change at the proper locations in the now more complex organization. It also becomes necessary to ensure that the proper people are involved and that the locations have the small and flexible nature that best encourages creativity and response to change. This often requires creating islands of garage shops in the midst of a bureaucracy.

How does one do this well? There are as many answers as there are innovative companies. However, there are some principles that tend to be rather general. Some fortunate companies have been able to retain an overall environment of innovation as they have grown to a large size. The rapidly growing electronic companies are good examples of this. The management has traditionally put a sizable fraction of the sales into R&D, and this money has been allocated at a reasonably low level on the organizational chart. The result has been involvement in R&D activities on the part of a large number of the engineers and, even more important, a high awareness of the nature and importance of innovation throughout the company. Creativity and change require the support of upper management and the understanding of the nature of the phenomenon at all levels.

Companies such as these have a relatively easy time in organizing and managing creative efforts. As discussed in Chapter 8, the resources may not always be allocated to the function with the problem (productivity and quality) and problems may occur in accepting the characteristics of increasing company size, but their tradition of strong and continuous innovation gives them an advantage in organizing and managing creativity and change over companies without such a tradition.

Railroad companies, for instance, have recently been thrust into more direct competition because of deregulation and they are finding that they do not have a tradition that lets them easily live with risk and experimentation. Steel companies in the United States offer another example of a situation where a tradition of creativity and responsiveness to change was lost with resulting competitive trauma.

ISLANDS AND GARAGE SHOPS

Organizational islands can be established to increase the creativity and ability to change within organizations, but the success of these islands depends on many factors. The islands must first of all be accepted in a realistic way by upper management. As we have mentioned repeatedly, creativity and change involve risk. In most organizations, there are managers who view the purpose of their jobs (life?) as ensuring that no "mistakes" are ever made. Organizational units existing as mechanisms for increasing creativity and ability to change must be somehow protected from this type of manager. Experiments sometimes fail. This is not to say that such units should not be tightly managed. However, they should be managed with an appreciation of the game they are being asked to play. More will be said about this later.

These islands must also have the reward systems and resources compatible with creativity and change, as we discussed earlier. There is also a distinct advantage in ensuring flexibility of these groups by either making them ad hoc in nature or rotating people through them. This has a double purpose. Activities such as research and development, preliminary design, and feasibility study can suffer if they become divorced from operations. Examples of this can sometimes be seen in large technology based companies where central R&D has attained its own separate location, budget, and cast of characters. It is possible for these units to wander continually toward the "R" and away from the "D" and finally lose their influence on the company. Operational managers (design, manufacturing, assembly) will view them as budget drains that do not understand the realities of the business. The managers of the increasingly independent think tanks will in turn think less and less about the intellectual acumen of the operations people.

These problems are minimized by utilizing a significant number of operations people (design, manufacturing, test) in R&D activities. For one thing, movement of personnel ensures that operations are represented in the islands and that the islands gain credibility when the operations people return to their primary responsibility. In addition, this movement results in a gain in morale (it is fun to work in R&D after a long hitch at project work) and creativity (it is a new mixture of thinking styles). Finally, movement of people stops stereotyping, which can hamper creativity and change in any organization. If a limited number of people are continuously identified with creativity and change, it is possible that the people and activities will lose effectiveness by being branded as "academic."

MANAGEMENT STYLE

Now let us discuss a related issue — management style or what is sometimes called influence style. Just as the organizational structure is important, so too is the way in which managers influence others.

In a sense, we all attempt to influence others, whether they be subordinates or superiors, family members, members of the community, people performing services for us, or people whom we serve. We attempt to do this in many ways.

If one reads management theory, one notes a tendency among management theorists to divide the world of management styles into two parts. Douglas McGregor perhaps best described this dichotomy when he coined the terms Theory X and Theory Y. The characteristics of Theory X and Theory Y are somewhat captured by the following words:

Theory X	Theory Y
Authority	Collaboration
Marine Corps.	University
One-way communication	Two-way communication
Auto assembly	R&D
Neat	Messy
Fast	Slow
Fun for boss	Fun for employee

It is worth diverging briefly into some comments on the evolution of management theory in the United States, since they shed some light on origins of Theory X and Theory Y. At the turn of the century, Theory X management was dominant. There was a proliferation of large organizations. Governments and armies grew enormously and, for the first time, large industries emerged. There was a vast market for manufacturing goods in the United States. There was also a large supply of highly motivated immigrant labor, and the agricultural revolution had displaced many people from the farm to the city. Labor unions were weak or nonexistent and the Protestant work ethic was strong.

Large factories utilizing techniques of mass production were becoming widespread. The workers were willing to put in long hours at low pay because they were trying to establish themselves and their families. Into this environment stepped a number of people (Frederick Taylor, Henry Fayol, Luther Gulick, Lyndall Urwick) who developed a theory of management called scientific management. This was Theory X incarnate.

However, in the 1930s, along with the industrial relations movement and the increasing numbers of psychologists becoming involved in business, Theory Y entered the scene. People realized that the output of workers can be improved by treating them as individuals rather than cogs in a machine. As time has passed, more and more management theorists have extolled the virtue of Theory Y considerations. Management theorists discovered such techniques as the leaderless sensitivity group (T-group) in the 1950s, and now write glowingly of the "organic," "informal," and "nonbureaucratic" organization. Peter Drucker's management by objective is a method whereby people are given objectives rather than detailed tasks. In this way they make use of their specific strengths and gain a greater sense of individual reward. Great attention has been focused on industrial democratization and the experimental assembly plants in Europe and the US, which utilize concepts such as team management, vertical integration, and employee ownership.

Let us consider Theory X (authority) and Theory Y (collaboration) in the context of the management of creativity and change. Theory Y has been the darling of the management theorists for the latter part of this century. It received a great boost when it appeared to be linked with the success of electronic and computer companies and when it became clear that it was an element in the amazing economic success of Japan. However, Theory X has not disappeared. It obviously still holds forth in the military. There is good reason for this. The military must remain stable despite a highly transient payroll and in time of war it is necessary to ask people to do things that they would probably not agree to do in a collaborative framework. It is also very much alive in many (if not most) industrial, governmental, and domestic organizations.

Theory X obviously has advantages or it would not have survived this long. In fact, an authoritative approach to management is somewhat natural in the western world. We were raised by authority and in fact tend to raise our children the same way. Most of you would expect your small child to "mind" you without involved deliberations or additional rewards.

Managing by authority is also fast and does not require subtle knowledge of the person being given the order or details of the situation. We tend to accept it, respect it, and admire the speed and dispatch with which it can accomplish certain things, as well we should. However, there are certain situations in which authority breaks down and, since we tend to resent taking orders a bit, we sometimes take advantage of its weaknesses. Authority must have a base. Much authority over small children is based on physical size. You may have become aware of this if you have had children who reached your size. The resulting disappearance of authority is called adolescence, and can be overcome only by rapidly moving the authority base to money. Authority can also be broken down by collective bargaining, as unions have learned.

Finally, in an organization, authority can be sabotaged very effectively if employees only do that which they are specifically asked to do. Perhaps this is one reason for the presently perceived quality problems in US manufacturing. Employees have been told which nuts to put on and how to put them on, but not how well to put them on. The recent passage of the Equal Opportunity Act, which requires equal pay for equal work, resulted in the propagation of detailed job descriptions since organizations were asked to be able to prove that in fact equal pay was being given for equal work. In many organizations, the preparation of these detailed descriptions caused the short-term loss of little things that had always been done on an informal basis. Detailed job descriptions not only outline what is to be done, but also imply what does not have to be done. Since few job descriptions say "makes the coffee," there may have been no coffee for a week or two.

This problem is critical in management of people who think for a living and are expected to be creative and respond to change. Creativity and change cannot be defined in detail, and authority just doesn't get the job done. If you order me to be more creative on the job and I resent you doing so, you are in trouble, not me. Although effective for many traditional tasks, Theory X management with its authority-based philosophy is not the proper way to manage if increased creativity and change are goals.

For creativity and change situations, collaboration is the clear winner. However, although collaborative management techniques are wonderful in situations involving creativity and change, they are not the universal management answer. There are situations in which the quickness and tidiness of authority is an advantage. The good manager should be able to mix management styles. This is not easy. Given a choice, would you rather be managed by Theory X or Theory Y? For most of us, that is an easy question to answer. Theory Y gives us much more challenge and satisfaction, and allows us to utilize our powerful intellect to the fullest. However, which theory would you prefer to use in managing others? Even the most enlightened of us define part of the management responsibility as "tidying up" the function that reports to us — as routinizing, ordering, standardizing. Such functions do have slight traces of Theory X. I am an obvious Theory Y manager. The institutions I prefer require it. However, I am continually confused when Theory Y does not result in the answer I want.

However, even if the collaborative process is less natural and requires more time and bickering, it results in improved implementation and, most importantly, it results in everyone buying into the responsibility to get the job done. This is exactly the way to increase my creativity — to hit me with the old "Gosh, we've got a problem" approach.

COMMUNICATING FOR CREATIVITY

In particular, the two-way communication involved with collaboration is essential to creativity and responsiveness to change. One-way communication is fast, appears orderly, and feels good to the sender. Dissemination of a memo concerning parking to all hands is immediate and gives one a feeling of great influence and accomplishment (for example, "Personnel will no longer park in the Building 29 loading dock area between the hours of 6:00 A.M. and 6:00 P.M."). There is only one problem. People will continue to park there. That is because, if you think back to earlier comments on the thinking process, that which is transmitted is not necessarily the same as that which is received. In this case, the message was probably submerged by a large number of personal considerations that the receiver added. The message that is received depends as much as what is (or is not) in our heads as on the message transmitted. Good communication requires a commonality of language as well as similar memory structures in the minds of the sender and the receiver. In the case of creativity and change, these structures are not as reliably similar as in situations of business as usual. It is worth diverging from our discussion to consider communication a bit more specifically because in situations involving creativity and change, communication is always critical. First of all, the process of dealing with original concepts requires communication across disciplines and related topics. Second, creativity and change require a great amount of "selling." In the selling process, outstanding communication is essential.

Communication requires a sender, a receiver, and a message. In order for it to be most effective, all three must use the same knowledge, priority, and value bases. The sender must encode the message in a form that will cause maximum attention and motivation on the part of the receiver, and the receiver must have time to properly decode the message. In addition, if high accuracy is to be obtained, feedback must be provided from the receiver back to the sender. Here is an exercise that lets us examine this process:

E X E R C I S E

Describe the following figure to someone while your back is turned to them and have them draw it. The rectangles are all twice as long as they are wide, their corners either touch nothing, other corners, or midpoints of the sides of other rectangles, and they are oriented either vertically, horizontally, or at 45 degrees. Tell the other person to give you no feedback and make no noise. This is one-way communication.

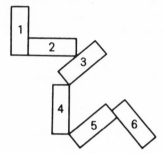

Now let us try two-way communication. Face the other person and describe the following similar figure allowing questions and discussion. Once again the person is to draw the figure.

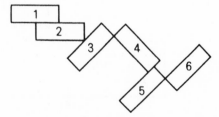

In neither case let them see the figure and confine yourselves to words (a dumb way to communicate some information, but a great favorite nonetheless).

You should have noticed several things. The two-way communication was probably more accurate. However, it was also probably slower and not as much fun for the sender. Had there been many receivers, this would have been even more evident, and frustration would have been higher because those who had gotten the message would be forced to sit and wait while the slower receivers completed the task. The one-way communication was probably not only quicker (although inaccurate), but also a more pleasant experience for the sender (unless there were snickers from the receiver). This is perhaps why our world is so full of memos.

I often use a game called "visual rumor" to demonstrate the in-accuracy of one-way communication to classes. In this game the first person in a line of ten or so is shown a simple drawing. After a bit of "study" time, the person describes the object in the drawing to the next, without allowing the second person to see the drawing. The object is subsequently passed down the line with verbal descriptions, and the last person draws it. Figure 11-2 shows a drawing of a simple object (it is an engineering drawing, but the people playing the game were students in an engineering class). Figure 11-3 shows some of the results. There was obviously some error.

One-way communication is amazingly weak in accuracy unless the receiver has the same information in mind as the sender. This is unlikely in situations involving creativity and change. Of course, the visual rumor task is also difficult because of the language problem.

FIGURE 11-2 The "Gizmo"

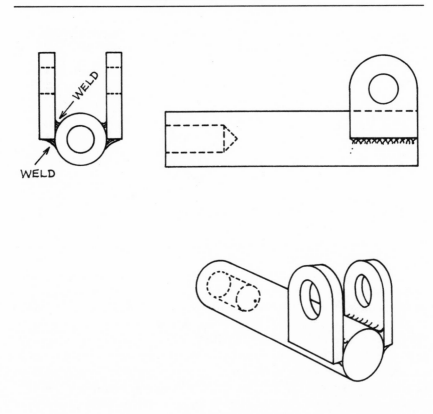

FIGURE 11-3 Visual Rumors of the "Gizmo"

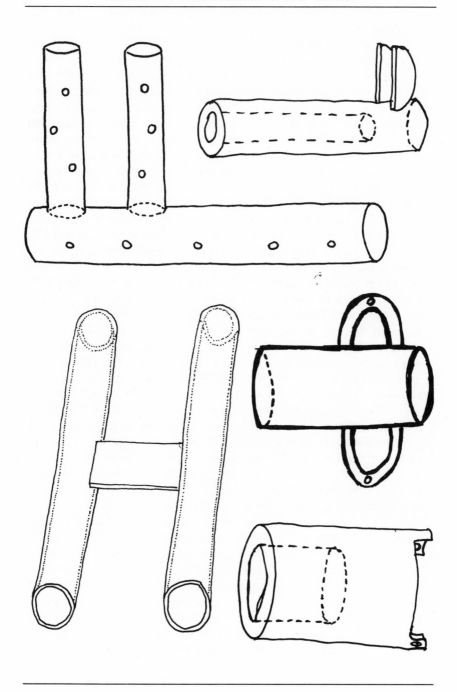

It forces people to deal verbally with physical forms, just as the rectangle exercise did. Physical forms should be dealt with graphically.

Why might communication difficulties occur in situations of creativity and change? First of all, in a business-as-usual situation, communication may be one-way. In situations where new directions are underway, one expects increased variance in the information, values, and priorities in different people's minds. Two-way communication, with resultant slowness and apparent messiness, becomes more important. This is consistent with what we have said in our discussion of management and organizational styles. If someone sends us a message we do not understand, we simply cannot do anything with it. We need the opportunity to work out the difficulties. If someone sends us a message we do not agree with, we will not do anything with it. Once again, we need the opportunity to reach agreement.

Also in situations of creativity and change, we may often combine disciplines in new ways. Communication across disciplines is unusually difficult because our mind is not particularly eager to learn new jargon and techniques, or to admit that we need to do so. We are afraid that our need to learn new information will be interpreted (mistakenly) as a sign of ignorance. One of the great challenges in teaching is that one cannot rely upon students to ask questions when they do not understand things. It is quite easy to lose an entire class (usually if one student does not understand, the others don't either) with no indication. One of the common explanations for this reluctance to ask questions is that asking questions is admitting ignorance.

I used to be called a systems engineer. When I was in the US Air Force, the military had just discovered the "systems" concept. No longer would there be an airplane, ammunition, starting carts, and a plug for the Pitot tube. Now there would be a weapon system. People began to talk in terms of the systems concept, systems management, systems approach, and, of course, systems engineering. Companies such as Ramo-Woolridge (the RW of TRW) leapt to prominence because of their systems design and management ability. This approach instantly infiltrated the aerospace industry, so that by the time I joined the Jet Propulsion Laboratory in 1959 it was known that a systems approach was necessary to design something as complex as a spacecraft. There was some dissension from certain senior people who considered systems engineering to be just plain old good engineering, but we youngsters leapt on it with enthusiasm. I was a systems engineer for a while at JPL and later taught systems engineering at Stanford and spent a large portion of my summers for ten years in a NASA-sponsored program, which attempted to give engineering professors a better feel for systems engineering.

What is systems engineering? Just plain old good engineering. However it has evolved its own philosophies and exists as a field because of the difficulty of communicating across different jargons, perceptions of importance, and perspectives in different technical fields. The communication engineers see nothing wrong with leaving an extra 3db margin in their system, even though some poor mechanical engineer may end up trying to design an antenna with twice the area as a result.

Interdisciplinary communication is not restricted to technological companies. Any organization has difficulties with communication between the various specialized groups within it, and any family has difficulty with communication between members exercising different roles in the family. The traditional housewife (should any still exist) has as much difficulty communicating with the traditional husband (none still exist), because of the difference in their experiences, perceived priorities, and responsibilities.

The message here is a simple but important one. In situations involving change and creativity, communication cannot be taken for granted. Efforts must be made to ensure that communications are two way and that adequate time and effort are taken to convey the information. It is also worthwhile to be suspicious as to difficulties due to changes in the disciplinary mix. Finally, priorities and values will perhaps need changing, and intensive communication is sometimes necessary to achieve this. In particular, a great amount of communication is required to convince people who have played a particular role for a long period of time to change their role.

THE DYNAMICS OF GROUPS

Why do crowds behave the way they do? Why do we act the way we do in groups? What are the forces that cause us to perceive situations, other people, and ourselves the way we do? Social psychologists produce striking demonstrations that our actions are strongly based on social bases as well as individual ones. Extrapolating to problem solving is difficult to avoid.

Take, for example, the now-familiar question of "getting involved." Social psychologists have experimented with situations involving physical welfare. In one situation, subjects were placed in individual booths and told that they would participate in a group discussion about personal problems by using an intercom. One of the subjects (a shill) mentioned that he had problems with seizures. At one point in the conversation he sounded as if he were about to begin a seizure. Some of the genuine subjects believed that the group consisted only of themselves and the subject with the seizure problem, others believed that it consisted of three people, and others that it consisted of six people. Eighty-five percent of the subjects who thought the group contained only two people reported the "seizure" to the person in charge of the experiments. Sixty-two percent of the subjects who thought the group consisted of three people reported it, and only 31 percent of those who thought the group included six spoke to the person in charge. The experiment was a demonstration of the dilution of our personal responsibility in groups.

If there is risk involved in problem solving, wouldn't one expect our participation in situations involving creativity and change to be similar? For us to be more interested in the solution of our own problems than of the social security problem? For us to become more involved if we think that we are one of a few working on a problem than one of many. This suggests that we should be careful not to overlook the individual. Rewards given for the success of a company will have less effect on individual performance than rewards given for the success of that individual. It says that psychological satisfaction will be more easily obtained in small groups and small companies instead of large ones.

THE "WHY DID I DO IT?" THEORIES

Pertinent to this book is the work that social psychologists have done in seeking to understand the forces that cause us to "go along." They speak about conforming to different degrees of influence. One of these is compliance, where we conform to satisfy our belonging needs even though we do not particularly believe the behavior or opinions that we profess. We do this routinely in social chitchat and in order to make favorable first impressions among strangers. If we do this consistently, we may internalize the role and come to believe it. In one psychology experiment college students were asked to work on an extraordinarily boring task for an hour. After completion, some of them were offered a dollar to tell the next subjects that the task had been fun. Others were offered twenty dollars to do the same thing. Later they were all asked how interesting the task really was. Figure 11-4 shows the result. Those given the small bribe apparently had come to believe that the task was relatively more interesting than the control students who were not bribed at all and not asked to tell others that it was interesting. The larger bribe was ineffective. What is going on? What is the process by which we internalize our compliance? These are questions important to the understanding of social behavior and the motivation of people.

FIGURE 11-4 Attitude Change and Incentive

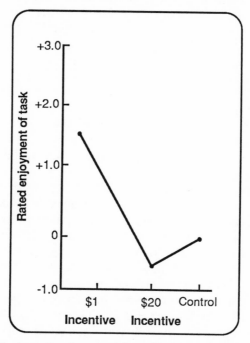

The smaller the incentive for complying with the experimenter's request, the greater the attitude change.

There are two theories that explain this, perhaps both related to Freud's rationalization. The older one, sometimes called the theory of cognitive dissonance, was first put forward by Leon Festinger in 1957. It hypothesizes that we are uncomfortable with cognitive conflicts. In the preceding case, we are uncomfortable with the coexistence of our experience with a dull task and our compliance with the request to describe it as fun. Therefore, we will choose one and eliminate the other. The theory of cognitive dissonance would explain the effects of the two magnitudes of bribes by telling us that the small bribe is an implication that the task really was fun or we wouldn't have complied with the request. The large bribe must have been a payment to lie, so the task was in fact boring.

The theory of cognitive dissonance received much attention in the 1960s when society was frantically attempting to understand the many apparent changes in values and actions of its citizens, especially its younger ones. It is still a wonderful theory to explain why we come to the conclusions we do. Cognitive dissonance tells us that if we sweat to make a decision, our memories adjust to validate our brilliance. It explains why the trauma of buying a house or choosing a college is later replaced by certainty that the choice was the right one. It explains why salespeople are better off if the customer has to think a bit before deciding on their product (return business is more likely). It explains why new car literature is read more by people after they buy the car. It explains why a year after a divorce an ex-mate of many years seems clearly insane.

The other theory is that of attribution. We are constantly called upon to attribute behavior (other people's or our own) to causes. According to attribution theory, we reach conclusions based on a number of rules. For instance, we tend to associate behavior with causes when there is a high correlation of the cause and the effect. We also tend, once we think we have a believable cause, to discount other ones. In the situation concerning the payment for the dull job, we might choose the most reasonable cause for our actions and discount the other ones. In the case of the high payment we would decide that anyone would have done the task for that money and discount other solutions. Therefore, we must have done it for the money, not because it was interesting. On the other hand, if the payment was low, the money is a less likely reason. We, therefore, cling to the reason that the job was interesting and discount the money.

Another pertinent psychological concept is that of identity with a reference group. According to this theory, we may change from compliance to internalization because we affiliate with a particularly important group of people who exhibit the particular behavior of attitudes. It is used to explain phenomena such as the conversion of Patty Hearst to a revolutionary and the conflict of school children between the values of their family (reference group #1) and their peers (reference group #2). This splitting occurs often and leave us in attitudinal conflict. We may want to identify both with devoted, dedicated, driving, single-minded executives and with sensitive, giving, family people. We may want to identify both with modern woman and traditional woman, with students and with senior faculty, or with the intellectual and the laid-back sensualist.

AD HOC GROUPS

Organizations large and small can benefit from the frequent use of ad hoc problem-solving groups. The desired problem-solving abilities can be provided, as we discussed in Chapter 6. The group will be highly motivated, since its very existence demonstrates the importance of the problem. Since it is not a permanent group, it will tend to be collaborative in nature. Because it is expected to be creative, it will be more tolerant of new directions. Finally, the group will bring long-term benefit to the organization by establishing understanding and communication between different areas.

I work with many ad hoc groups, either as consultant or member, and I find them remarkably productive insofar as creativity and change are concerned. Surprisingly enough, I find their use more common in very large organizations (governments, industry) than in small organizations. Many organizations such as schools, museums, community action groups, and even large families could make good use of ad hoc groups representing varied interests to work on specific problems. Such groups can operate in a truly creative manner, since they are not anchored to past traditions and constraints. If they contain (ideally) or are supported by those in the organization who control resources and make policy decisions, they can accomplish a great deal.

GROUP CREATIVITY TECHNIQUES

Let us examine two popular group creativity techniques in order to gain an appreciation of how groups can be constrained to act in a way that promotes creativity. Brainstorming, which has been mentioned several times, is perhaps the most well-known of all group creativity techniques. Its invention is attributed to Alex Osborn, one of the founders of the advertising firm of Batten, Barten, Durstine, and Osborn. It has four rules.

1. Absolutely no evaluation
2. Wildest possible ideas
3. As many ideas as possible
4. Build upon other ideas

A typical brainstorming group involves five to ten people, operates completely democratically, and exhibits a relatively manic style. It should have a recorder to write down ideas and involve at least one person who is a stranger to the problem. It may proceed for twenty or thirty minutes before it runs out of steam. If it stops too soon, it will merely have exhausted the obvious alternatives; if it continues too long, it will lose its momentum.

It is not as simple as it seems to follow these rules. The rule against evaluation even prohibits statements such as "Did you say . . . .?" delivered with raised eyebrows. In fact, the group should be complementary toward outrageous ideas. Humor obviously should be present, but the group should remain intensely focused on the problem. Finally, the final rule is difficult to remember. Building on previously suggested ideas both compliments the original author of the idea and continually bends wild concepts toward practicality. However, brainstorming tends to reward people on the basis of their individual submissions to the process, so that the tendency is for people to put their energy into inventing new concepts rather than building on existing ones.

The brainstorming process always works. However, it has several shortcomings. It does not include mechanisms for converging that are as powerful as the mechanisms for divergence. Groups, therefore, tend to revert to conservatism and judgment in convergence and throw out much of the creativity they have generated. When I use brainstorming, I usually ask the group to select a number of favorite concepts, perhaps the most practical, the most exciting, and the most outrageous. I will then try to keep one or two alive that are in the middle of the range. Brainstorming works beautifully in the advertising business (where it was invented) because those involved seem to share a sense for potentially successful concepts. Also, the advertising business values raw concepts highly. However, it is more difficult to use in situations involving high degrees of disciplinary expertise and complex implementation processes.

This leads us to brainstorming's other great weakness: it is somewhat shallow in its ability to handle expertise. If no evaluation is possible, it is difficult to include experts, whose function in life may be to say things like "A molecule like that is physically impossible." In complex situations, it is a good technique when a broad direction or a narrow fix is needed, but less effective when a maze of coordinated details may be involved. It is not too much fun to brainstorm the structural details of a suspension bridge.

THE SYNECTICS APPROACH

Synectics offers an interesting contrast. It was developed by Synectics Inc., in Boston, Massachusetts. It is not as easy to learn as brainstorming. Typically it requires a commitment of several days and considerable dollars and a professional trainer. This is one of the reasons it is not as widespread as brainstorming. Synectics Inc. has been studying creative problem solving for a large number of years. It has concluded that the problem is not so much producing a concept but rather allowing a group to interact in a way that the final solution will be implemented. The technique is therefore client-centered. The founders of the technique feel that only the person with the problem is going to implement a solution and that the best that the problem-solving group can hope for is to inspire this person. The technique strives to give the client a new direction.

The leader of a Synectics group is a facilitator and a recorder only. He or she is not allowed to directly input the problem-solving process. Although Synectics pays a penalty for this (leaders like to input), they could think of no other way to guarantee that the leader would not dominate the process. A Synectics group contains five to ten people, including experts and nonexperts, and a session continues for about 45 minutes.

Synectics training makes heavy use of videotape in order to teach people to recognize group actions that are positive and negative to creative problem solving. Figures 11-5 and 11-6 are from a paper by George Prince, the founder of Synectics Inc. They categorize actions

FIGURE 11-5 Actions That Lead to Creative Problem Solving

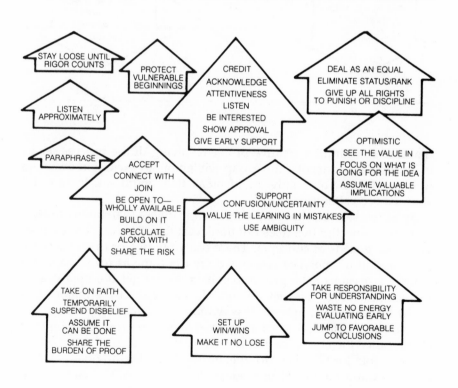

FIGURE 11-6 Actions That Inhibit Creative Problem Solving

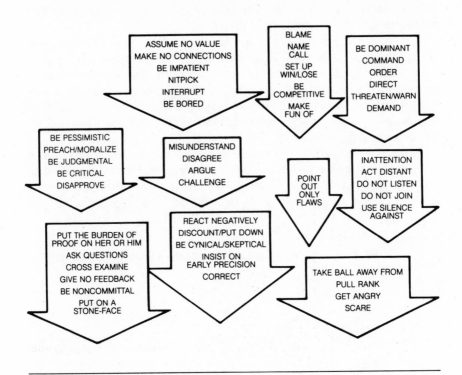

that lead to or inhibit creative problem solving. If the process seems to be short on concepts, the group will go on an excursion designed to generate new alternatives and break their mind set. Figure 11-7 shows a typical excursion.

Synectics sessions have a different atmosphere than brainstorming sessions. Synectics Inc. does not think that the client can successfully deal with dozens of concepts. Therefore, only two or three ideas are generated at a time. The sessions do not become as manic as brainstorming sessions. The group members do not get the opportunity to gain satisfaction by their fluency. In fact, one of the major tasks of the leader is to suppress ideas without discouraging participants. The group must also learn to gain satisfaction from pleasing the client. Since the client has the last word at each step of the process, it is possible for the client to operate solely on the original problem statement and his or her own ideas. In such cases, the group must

FIGURE 11-7 A Synectics Excursion

1. Leader asks client to select a directional Goal/Wish for which he/she'd like to develop Innovative Possible Solutions.
2. Leader picks a key word (action, concept) from the Goal/Wish.
3. Leader asks group (including client) to think of an example of that key word (action, concept) from a world that is distant from the world of the problem. The leader chooses the world. The leader then writes up a list of the group's examples.
4. Leader asks group to forget about the problem and the Goal/Wish and focus on any of the listed examples, thinking about its associations, images it conjures up, etc. Group members are asked to note these down on individual pads.
5. Leader asks group to use all or part of their example material to develop an Absurd Idea (probably impractical, impossible, or illegal) that addresses the original Goal/Wish.
6. Leader asks group to develop second generation ideas from any one of the Absurd Ideas (extracting key principles and applying them in a more realistic fashion without diluting the innovation).
7. Leader asks client to pick an idea that has appeal from the second generation ideas.
8. Process proceeds with paraphrase back to the original problem and itemized response from the client.

get satisfaction from the satisfaction of the client and not become frustrated when they think the client exhibits poor judgment.

The Synectics approach integrates many principles of creative problem solving. The problem is carefully investigated. Alternate wordings are presented to the client by the group in order to ensure that the statement really is consistent with the difficulty. Interestingly enough, the client will often prefer an alternate statement. Synectics also makes heavy use of what is called an "itemized response." In such a response, two positive comments are made before a reservation. The two positive comments are intended to reward the authors of the idea and to give the group additional opportunity to understand the client's desires. The reservation is a chance for criticism (another difference from brainstorming). Synectics is not a totally divergent process. In fact, it is a process that continues to improve one of two or three original concepts. It does not return to "go" after an original direction is selected.

Both brainstorming and Synectics take advantage of many of the principles discussed in this book. The proper makeup of a group ensures the human resources necessary for solving the problem, since the groups are usually somewhat ad hoc and the necessary specializations can be included. The existence of the group ensures that time is spent on the generation of alternate concepts. There are heavy psychological rewards for the members of the group in both cases. The local culture is changed to one in which belonging is accomplished by being creative. Both groups make use of creativity techniques in themselves. Of particular interest is the Synectics analysis of the problem. In addition, Synectics training includes setbreakers and other techniques so that if concept generation is ever an obstacle (which it usually is not), a diversion to a creativity technique can be taken. Finally, both brainstorming and Synectics utilize completely informal organization and an entirely collaborative management style. Bosses are not allowed to dominate the process and all members are made to feel equally valuable and are encouraged to participate. This is consistent with the main message of this chapter in that organizational and management styles are highly influential in situations involving creativity and change.

Informal, small collaborative groups representing a wide range of disciplines tend to be highly creative and able to adapt to change easily. However, formal large groups with considerable specialization and authority are excellent for other purposes. Large organizations typically must contain a wide range of organizational and management styles to ensure creativity and responsiveness to change in the right place at the right time. To expect a large and complex organization to remain healthy without conscious effort being spent on providing appropriate structures and influence styles for creativity and change is as foolish as attempting to turn it into one giant garage shop. This is an important consideration, since effort is required to attain the advantages of both bigness and smallness. This principle is often conveniently overlooked. The next chapter will discuss decision making and a few strategic considerations of value in the management of creativity and change. The line between strategy and tactics is always a fuzzy one because the boss's tactic may be the employee's strategy. However, there are certainly high-level concerns in any organization that are critical in either encouraging or inhibiting creativity and the ability to change. The next chapter will talk about a few of them.

12

Decision Making
and Strategy

Let us complete this book by devoting a chapter to two topics not often considered in books about creativity and change — decision making and strategy. It does us no good to consciously override our habits and deviate from business as usual if we then kill our new directions by traditional techniques of judgment. It is useless to desire new directions if our strategic thinking then resists them. The topics we have been discussing in this book not only make it difficult to deviate but also cause us to take a somewhat habitual approach to decision making and the strategies we use in problem solving. In situations requiring increased creativity or ability to change, decision making and strategy are critical, and we need to worry about whether our efforts in these directions are consistent with attaining our desired goals. As before, we must resort to use of our conscious in order to do so.

THE NATURE OF DECISION MAKING

Decision making is central to problem solving. The convergent thinking associated with decision making is no less critical than the divergent thinking associated with the production of concepts, since any concept can be killed either by an early decision that it is not acceptable or a later decision that it is too costly to implement. As previously mentioned, perhaps the main weakness of the technique of brainstorming is that it is concerned only with the production of ideas, not the decisions involved in converging the resulting list to the prime contender(s). Brainstorming temporarily changes the culture of the group to be highly productive at a conceptual level. However, when the results are contemplated in the cold light of normalcy, many of the benefits of the brainstorming process end up on the cutting room floor.

Once again, if we suspect that our problem-solving habits (in this case, decision making) are not consistent with creativity and change, we must become more conscious in our thinking. How can we do this with regard to decision making? One way, of course, is to become more aware of the forces that bias decisions in conservative and traditional directions, and attempt to compensate. We can try to remember that new concepts are delicate and that we must modify our usual tough-minded judgmental style. However this may not be adequate, because our habits are sometimes stronger than our good intentions.

Another approach is to make use of structures that motivate us to be more consciously thoughtful of not only our goals but also of the risks and potential benefits and costs of our decisions. Insights into these structures come from examining presently existing formal decision-making techniques. This may seem strange, because these approaches are usually thought to be, if anything, less creative and flexible than the usual unstructured approach we take to decision making. However, they do cause one to think more consciously about decisions and, in situations involving creativity and change, that is an advantage. I tend to view all problem-solving techniques as aids and do not look to any of them for the right answer. If the problem is of importance, there is no "right" answer. I therefore do not expect decision-making techniques to make the decision for me. However, they do make me think of what I am attempting to do and remind me of difficult considerations that my efficient mind would otherwise consign to the unconscious.

We make many of our decisions based on an unconscious mix of experience and emotion. Our mind is very good at integrating the complexities involved with little conscious intervention. This is the type of decision involved in making "snap judgments" of people. When we decide to see a movie, order from McDonald's, buy a book, or choose a greeting card, we do not use formalized methods to make our choice — we just do it. This unconscious approach to problem solving is sometimes called "hunching" and is not confined to minor decisions. We tend to also rely heavily on our unconscious when we buy houses or cars, decide to have babies, pick mates, and choose whether or not to have elective surgery.

This intuitive decision-making capability is near and dear to us, as well it should be, because it is based on our life experience and knowledge. It does not bog us down in the search for the one right answer, which is good because decisions are usually so complex that the one right answer does not exist. It is a profoundly powerful ability that almost automatically considers preferences, unknowns, probabilities, and data. However, like other highly automatic mental processes, it is based highly on precedent and is quite conservative. I would conjecture that in most cases it is exactly what we want. However, it is not necessarily consistent with increasing creativity or ability to change. Unconscious decision making is habitual and, therefore, may destroy new directions. Our inherent love of Quarter-Pounders may forever deprive us of Chicken McNuggets.

PRIORITIZING CRITERIA

Let us consider a few existing decision structures to see how they cause us to think more consciously about our decisions. The simplest form of structure we can inject into decision making is probably the prioritized use of criteria, such as the one shown in Table 12-1, which I recently used in deciding what grades to assign the 120 papers written by students in a class I am teaching.

TABLE 12-1 Prioritized Criteria for Paper Grading

Thorough analysis	20 points
Specific and personal	10 points
Reflects course	10 points
Imaginative and well-written	10 points

The paper involved a self-analysis of problem-solving ability in a context similar to that of this book. However, I had told the students that I wanted the analyses to be specific and personal, to reflect the material we had covered in the course, and to be imaginative and well-written. I had, in fact, given this list of criteria when I gave them the assignment and used it to remind myself to make my grading decisions in this particular way. It was also helpful as I tried to grade somewhat uniformly across 120 papers (a next-to-impossible task). Prioritized criteria are often used in design reviews of projects, admission of college students, and purchase of investments for personal portfolios. They simply allow one to detail decision priorities more specifically than pure intuition might do and to "rig" them in a direction somewhat at odds with one's unconscious tendencies. They are valuable because in addition to having to think consciously about whether such criteria are fulfilled, we have to do quite a bit of conscious work in coming up with the criteria in the first place. In the case of Table 12-1, the prioritized criteria helped me grade "creatively," in that the result was different from that ordinarily expected of an engineering professor. I could as easily design a list of criteria to make sure that I did not throw away all of the unusual ideas from a brainstorming session.

THE T-CHART AND DECISION MATRIX

Another simple structure is the T-chart shown in Figure 12-1. This is a format to ensure that attention is paid to potential good news and bad news that may result from a particular decision. The format encourages conscious thought on possible benefits and losses from a new direction. The blankness of the format encourages us to write a lot, and some strange desire for symmetry may cause us to worry if the list of negatives is appreciably longer than the list of positives.

Another structural approach is the use of a decision matrix. As a trivial example, suppose we need to purchase an automobile, and a

FIGURE 12-1 A T-chart

POSITIVES	NEGATIVES

reading of the want ads shows eight interesting possibilities. The matrix requires that we be specific about the qualities we want in our car, their relative priority to us and, if possible, their relative values. It will have the cars listed in the rows, and the columns will be devoted to the qualities of interest in the decision. In each space in the columns will be the relative rank of each car. If we wanted to be particularly rigorous, we would weight each quality of interest in accordance with its importance to us. Our matrix might look like the one in Table 12-2 (high numbers are better).

TABLE 12-2 A Decision Matrix for Buying a Used Car from the Want Ads

Car	Mechanical condition (x2)	Aesthetic appeal (x3)	Interior condition (x1)	Price (x3)	Life expect. (x2)	Total
'76 Nissan	7 (14)	4 (12)	5 (5)	5 (15)	6 (12)	58
'72 Ford	1 (2)	2 (6)	1 (1)	8 (24)	1 (2)	35
'59 Cad	4 (8)	8 (24)	3 (3)	4 (12)	5 (10)	57
'82 Jag	5 (10)	7 (21)	6 (6)	1 (3)	3 (6)	46
'71 MG	2 (4)	5 (15)	2 (2)	3 (9)	2 (4)	34
'67 Cam	3 (6)	6 (18)	4 (4)	2 (6)	4 (8)	42
'79 Colt	6 (12)	1 (3)	7 (7)	7 (21)	7 (14)	57
'80 Chev	8 (16)	3 (9)	8 (8)	6 (18)	8 (16)	67

The matrix tells us to buy the 1980 Chevrolet. A normal reaction at this point might be that we do not want the 1980 Chevrolet; we want the 1959 Cadillac. However, that is all right. Decision techniques do not make decisions, they simply assure that the decision maker has consciously analyzed the situation. Filling out the matrix makes us do that. We are still allowed to add a bit of unconscious to the mix.

DECISION ANALYSIS

An even more structured approach to decision making is probabilistic decision analysis, sometimes called simply decision analysis. In this approach, a tree is drawn that represents decision options. Each node, or junction, is a decision point at which the decision maker must decide to take one of the available paths. For each path a value must be assigned, as well as the probability of that value being achieved. For instance, we might need to decide whether our three-year-old daughter's birthday party should be inside or out. If the weather is sunny, we would like it to be outside. In fact, that would be the most favorable outcome. However, if it rained, an outside party would be a disaster. An inside party would work in the rain, but an inside setup would not be optimal if it did not rain. Let us assign some values. Let us say that the value of an outside party in the sun is 10. The value of an outside party in the rain is 0. An inside party in the rain is worth 6. An inside party with the sun shining is worth 2.

We now have to set the probability of rain. That is up to us. We can use the newspaper or our own estimate. Let us say that the paper says that the probability of rain is 0.4, but we do not believe it. We think that it is low, so we choose 50 percent. Our simple tree is shown in Figure 12-2. Looks as though we should have an outside party.

Decision analysis, of course, is usually applied to more complicated situations. Figure 12-3 is a grown-up example of a decision tree.

FIGURE 12-2 A Decision Analysis of Whether to Hold a Party Indoors or Outdoors

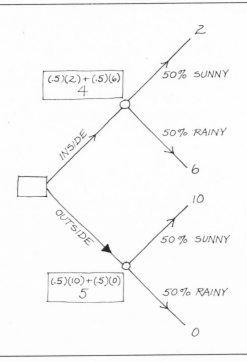

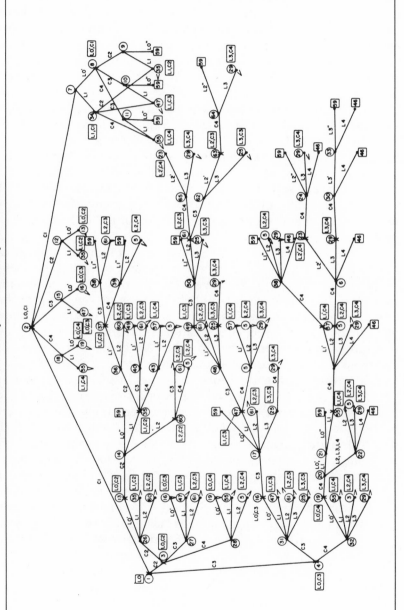

FIGURE 12-3 An Analysis of a Complex Decision

Decision analysis often annoys people for several reasons. One is a perception that it is meant to replace the usual type of intuitive unconscious decision making. This is simply not true. It is an aid that ensures conscious thinking during decision making. Its practitioners do not claim that it is intended to replace hunching. Decision analysis is intended to augment it. However, it seems to be threatening enough to many people who pride themselves on their decision-making ability that they insist on thinking that it is intended to do so.

Secondly, it is criticized because it simplifies the decision-making situation. Any analytical technique that is applied to life must simplify the situation because otherwise the technique would simply be too cumbersome to use. Finally, it annoys people because of the necessity of fixing values and probabilities. In complex situations, decision makers will often claim that it is impossible to set these. However, advocates of decision analysis will argue that it is foolish to make decisions without a clear appraisal of the value of alternate possibilities.

As for probability, decision analysis asks for numbers that are the most reasonable to the decision maker. In some occasions, these may be based on firm data. However, usually they are a quantitative estimate. There are even aids to help decision makers set probabilities. One of these is called a probability wheel. Figure 12-4 shows one version. It has a pointer that can be spun and a colored segment that can be adjusted to cover from 0 to 360 degrees of the wheel. I might ask you the odds of a major trend change in the stock market (say 300 points in the Dow Jones average) in the next six months. You might claim that you couldn't possibly place a probability on that. I would then set the colored area at something like 95 percent of the wheel and ask you whether you would rather have $1,000 if the stock market made a major change in the next six months or if the spinner of the wheel landed in the colored zone when I spun it. You would probably choose the spinner. I would then close the colored area down to 1 percent and ask you the same question. You would probably choose the stock market. I would then close in on you, alternately increasing and decreasing the size of the colored zone until you would become indifferent between the spinner and the stock market. You might exhibit discomfort while we were doing this, but I could probably find a probability that would be both indifferent in your judgment and very sensitive, in that a change of a few percent would destroy the equality.

Decision analysis, like matrices, T-charts, and ranked criteria lists, encourages conscious thinking during decision making. I tend to use

FIGURE 12-4 A Probability Wheel

these techniques in situations involving creativity and change, because even though they are extremely "left brain," they do cause
conscious attention to be paid to the decisions that are being made
and, therefore, to their affect on creativity and change. I even defend
expert programs from people who claim that they are dangerous
because they make creativity and change less likely. Granted, they
cannot at present duplicate the intuitive leaps made by people. However, they do shed light on the process of decision making and cause
us to become more conscious of the process.

If you are not familiar with expert programs, they are computer-
based decision-making models of experts. Once again, they do not
replace experts, they merely replicate certain problem-solving processes used by the experts. The process of designing such programs

includes detailed questioning of the expert in order to define specifically the heuristics (judgments) made by the expert in problem situations. These rules are combined with knowledge and then the resulting programs are made available to the expert. Typically these programs contain several hundred heuristic rules and a large amount of data. They are interactive and can be queried if the user takes issue with them. They are presently in use in many fields, including medicine, biochemistry, computer design and development, and petroleum production.

Now certainly an expensive computer-based expert program adds rigidity to decision making over long time periods because of the investment, the difficulty of changing it, and the dependence that users acquire. Why should it help creativity and change? First of all, the design of the program sheds light on the way in which decisions are made, and any awareness of this process helps. Second, to date, most professional people fight these programs, both philosophically and specifically. I am in charge of a two-week executive program for engineering managers. I have from time to time presented segments to them in both decision analysis and expert systems. Their response is the same. They find the people making the presentations arrogant (even though they are not) and are quick to point out that they themselves certainly could not be "replaced by a machine" (even though no one said they could be). In fighting these programs, people tend to think consciously about the decision-making process and in doing so become less habitual. In fact, in situations involving creativity and change, there could be no better challenge to decision makers than to prove that they are not machines.

KEPNER-TREGOE

A final example of a decision-making technique is that of Kepner-Tregoe, widely taught in industry over the past years. The philosophy of this technique is contained in *The New Rational Manager*, a book by Charles H. Kepner and Benjamin B. Tregoe. Figure 12-5 outlines the process. The manager must first of all identify areas of difficulty. These are then separated, made more specific, and prioritized. One of three analytical schemes is then chosen. If the problem is not precisely defined, the Problem Analysis is begun (bottom of Figure 12-5). In this process, difficulties are examined in order to specify the exact problem. Possible causes are then generated and each is tested against the problem specification. The most probable cause is then verified in the work environment.

FIGURE 12-5 The Kepner-Tregoe Technique for Decision Making

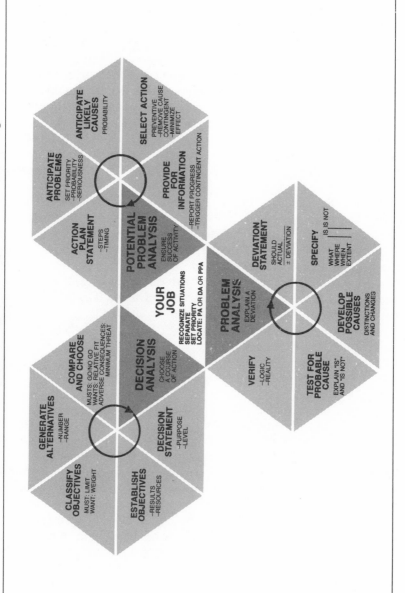

If the problem is defined, the manager chooses the Decision Analysis (the left-hand portion of Figure 12-5). In this process, a concise statement of purpose is expanded into objectives for defining the achievement of that purpose. These objectives are then prioritized as to importance. Alternate possibilities are then generated and compared using the criteria. The most favorable is selected. Should the problem already be defined and the decision chosen and implemented (and therefore the problem solved), the manager may select the Potential Problem Analysis. This is a process of formally thinking about future problems, isolating the most potentially harmful, and preventing them from occurring. It begins with identifying areas of vulnerability. Specific problems are identified within these areas, and actions are identified that will prevent occurrence of the potential problems. If they cannot be prevented, actions are chosen that will minimize them.

Kepner-Tregoe, like the techniques previously discussed, is a highly left-brained approach to problem solving. It formalizes a process that often operates largely in the unconscious. However, its proponents rightly claim that it results in creativity. It is another example of a problem-solving technique that causes us consciously to question our traditional intuitive decision making. It forces us to analyze our habits and in the process we may override or even change them.

STRATEGY AND CREATIVITY

Let us now spend some time discussing strategy. If we are interested in the management of creativity and change, we must consider the role that strategy plays. A strategy is a plan to reach our goals cleverly. While it is sometimes possible to reach goals in a muddling and fatalistic way, there are advantages in thinking strategically, in using forethought, and in combining tactics as skillfully as possible.

Strategic thinking and planning are intimately connected with creativity and change. First of all, strategic thinking itself is a creative act. For most of us, strategic thinking is not automatic. It is a divergence from business as usual and not easy, since it causes us to confront the large uncertainties associated with the future. Most of us are aware that we should be thinking strategically about our personal lives. Those of us who do tend to accomplish our goals more readily. The following exercise brings you up against the thought processes necessary to do so. Contemplate it. You do not even have to complete it unless you want to.

E X E R C I S E (O P T I O N A L)

Choose one of your personal goals that is important to you. Write a strategic plan to accomplish this goal. A few pages should be sufficient. Make sure your plan is chronological with specific dates, includes required resources, and confronts both the necessary interactions with other people and the activities you will have to sacrifice in order to reach this goal.

Whether you do this exercise or not, you may realize that it is not only potentially beneficial but also not your usual way of thinking. Most of us would just as soon avoid setting precise goals and avoid the type of problem solving associated with strategic thinking.

For a number of years I taught a course entitled Introduction to Engineering at Stanford. The students in the course were typically freshmen and sophomores and were somewhat interested in engineering as a major and as a profession. The class was oriented toward helping them better understand the nature of engineering. Typically, the most traumatic assignment for them was the one I considered the most useful. They were asked to choose the field of engineering that most appealed to them and then to write a paper detailing a typical working day in their life six months out of school, five years out of school, and fifteen years out of school. It was traumatic because they were not used to dealing with future uncertainties and because the paper indirectly asked them to think about their future goals. In a sense, it asked them to reflect upon the strategy of their life.

Not only is strategic thinking creative, but it also results in plans that require creativity to implement and result in change. Strangely enough, one of the often-heard arguments against strategic planning in organizations is based on the viewpoint that plans inhibit creativity and change. This is the opportunistic argument, which maintains that if one is committed to a plan and a strategy, one will be less likely to respond to opportunities as they come along. In my mind, this is a specious argument, often used to mask a more central factor — namely, that the people making the argument simply do not like thinking about strategy and the future. It is exactly because of the need to effectively manage creativity and change that strategic thinking and planning are necessary. The problem of being locked into a paper plan should not be real for anyone who understands the process of human problem solving.

As we join in complex endeavors requiring larger numbers of individuals, strategic thinking becomes even more important. I make that statement realizing that strategic planning in business is presently more controversial than it was a few years ago. However, this controversy arose because of the style in which planning was done, not because of the concept of planning. In the 1970s, a strong emphasis on strategic planning was the rage in businesses in the United States. Most large organizations pursued formal planning efforts, often with formal planning staffs, planning directors, and planning offices. Consultants in strategic planning abounded. However, toward the end of the 1970s, skepticism began to rear its head. In 1980, a book entitled *Strategies for Change* was written by James Quinn, a professor at the Amos Tuck School of Business at Dartmouth University. In an early passage, he had this to say:

"As time went on, however, I noticed three disturbing tendencies. First, the planning activity often tended to become a bureaucratized, rigid, and costly paper-shuffling exercise. In many companies, its primary impact was to expand the scope of capital and operational budgeting procedures, to introduce formal measures to new areas of performance, and thus to achieve greater central control over operations. Instead of stimulating creative options, innovation, or entrepreneurship, formal planning often became just another aspect of controllership — and another weapon in organizational politics. Second, most major strategic decisions seemed to be made outside the formal planning structure, even in organizations with well-accepted planning cultures. This tendency was especially marked in entrepreneurial and smaller enterprises. As I observed my client companies over long time periods, however, it became increasingly apparent that this was also a characteristic of good management in large organizations and not an abrogation of some immutable management principle. Third, much of the management literature on planning seemed bent on developing ever more sophisticated models of a system that simply was not working the way the model builders thought it was — or should be — operating. In fact, their purported "normative" solutions began to appear highly questionable, if not actively destructive, in many instances."

Note that Quinn is not against planning, he is merely against the type of formal planning that tends to become a separate activity utilized by various managers for political purposes rather than by all management for accomplishing organizational goals. He is opposed to planning that results in new staff positions and impressive bound documents rather than change in the organizations. In his book, he advocates an incremental approach to planning based on his study of how changes actually occur.

STRATEGIC THINKING AS A CREATIVE ACTIVITY

Since strategic thinking and planning are creative activities, the messages of this book apply to the process. If we are attempting to reach a state other than our present one, we must be suspicious of our traditional habits of thinking. We need to ensure good perception of the present and good prediction of the future. This means that we have to be conscious of the role that our personal priorities, desires, and values are playing. We all attempt to influence life in a way that is consistent with our personal priorities, desires, and values. However, we do not want to let them get us into trouble.

In large organizations, one of the responsibilities of managers is to look for signs that new directions are necessary. This is an extremely difficult perceptual problem. It is easy to find historical situations in which personal values impeded this process. Examples abound in the industries where the Japanese picked up commanding market share in the 1960s and 1970s. Part of their success was due to a post-World War II attitude on the part of many managers in the United States that the Japanese were unimaginative and just not capable of competing with the United States. Such attitudes also slowed downsizing of automobiles and computers. It is difficult to recognize signals that conflict with one's own values (large cars and mainframes are better). When designing strategy, one should always remain aware of the cognitive and social forces that tend to bias problem solving toward the traditional. A basic reason for the existence of strategic planning is that traditions change.

Like other forms of creative thinking, the process of strategic thinking and planning requires a reward system and resources consistent with the activity. This is good justification for the off-site retreat so familiar to business participants. It requires a broad, fresh data base. Consultants or other people representing outside opinion and values are an important resource in such activities because of the breadth of perspective and alternatives they provide.

The appropriate organizational and management style is also necessary in the process of strategic thinking and planning. Strategic planning must take place at many levels in organizations. A strategy only at the top management level has little chance for success unless it is reflected in strategies at the working level and vice versa. An

organization should have strategic plans at the functional level —
marketing strategy, manufacturing strategy, financial strategy, R&D
strategy, and so on. It should also have strategies corresponding to
business units, whether they be product (or service) families, plants
in different locations, profit centers, or different companies operating
under a parent organization. Finally, it should have strategies at the
parent, corporation, institutional, or other top level.

There is quite a bit of discussion among those involved in strategic
thinking as to whether strategy should be top-down (created by top
management and promulgated throughout the organization) or bottom-up (created by those involved in the detailed work of producing
the product or service). The answer, of course, if you believe what I
have been talking about in this book, is both. Since creativity and
change are involved, two-way communication is needed to ensure
accuracy and the integration of concepts from all quarters. Participatory management is needed in the compilation of strategy in order
to ensure that the result is realistic, that it is imaginative, and that it
can be easily implemented. For the same reasons, the creation of
strategy needs an ad hoc informal organizational style. Strategic planning is creative problem solving oriented toward change. A strong
bottom-up component is therefore needed in its development.

On the other hand, strategy must reflect the type of overall concerns that are the responsibility of top management. It must also
have total commitment from top management. As we have seen,
change is difficult and new directions are accompanied by natural
resistance, unforeseen resource needs, and risk. Top management
must be willing to accept this risk and ensure that the costs are paid.
Top management must also ensure that its policies are integrated
into strategic planning and be responsible for the implementation of
the plan.

Attention must also be paid to communication in the strategic
thinking and planning activity. Since new concepts are being dealt
with and new combinations of people are interacting, communication
should be two-way, informal, and thorough. Education is sometimes
needed in new areas pertinent to new goals, and old decision habits
should be suspect. Finally, techniques may be useful in the process.
Techniques are available for strategic planning just as they are for
increasing creativity. This is not a book on strategic planning so none
of them will be detailed here. The next and final chapter includes
several excellent books on strategic planning that will refer the interested reader to additional material.

Many consulting firms and individual consultants specialize in the
area of strategic planning. The available techniques are similar to
those available for increasing creativity because they work, but they
work better for some organizations, groups, and individuals than for

others. They are based upon sound premises and, if these premises are understood, it is possible to plan without importing specific techniques, often with results that have a better fit and therefore are more implementable.

STRATEGIC THINKING AS AN AGENT OF CHANGE

Let us now say a few words about some features of strategic thinking and planning that can increase the odds of their becoming reality. Plans are, after all, a recipe for future change and creativity. Although shelves of plans that will have little influence might have been tolerated in the 1970s, they fortunately no longer are. In order to ensure that plans are implemented, it is helpful to consider the problems of implementing them during the planning process and to ensure that the necessary mechanisms will be available. What habits will need to be changed? What will be necessary to change them? Reward systems must be provided during the implementation so that individuals will accommodate to new roles and activities. Resources must be made available for experimentation and new directions. Organizational and management styles may require change during the implementation and beyond. Strategic thinking should finally consider whether explicit provisions must be made for new communication links and techniques, education and training, and decision-making structures.

It is also necessary to understand the present situation *and* the transient state as well as the desired future state. This may sound obvious, but I have seen many situations where the goal was specified in great detail and the transient state was ignored. Implementation is likely to be smoother if we understand where we are and how we got there as well as where we want to be. In particular, effort should be spent on the details of transitions. We will be well served not only by knowing what we want to accomplish over time, but also by being able to answer questions such as the following in detail:

Who will be involved? Who will it be necessary to have committed to new directions and when? Who will be responsible for what functions at what time and who will report to whom during the transitions?

Where will the transition first take place? In the effected units? In new units specifically put together for the purpose? In the staff? In first-line management?

What changes will be needed in the organization? In management style? In personnel? In ad hoc and temporary groups?

Strategic plans are also more likely to become reality if they consider contingencies — at least the best and the worst possible guesses of the future. As well as planning on the likely sales level of a proposed product, shouldn't we also consider the worst possible sales level and the best? It would give us more perspective and give us a better indication of how much risk we were dealing with. As previously mentioned, I am a firm believer in confronting risk as directly as possible. Direct consideration of contingencies not only gives a more rational indication of probable future bounds but also makes it less likely that anyone will start confusing the plans with reality.

Finally, it is worthwhile to design an evaluation plan to aid implementation. Periodic feedback measuring progress against goals provides reward, enables corrections, and ensures that old habits do not regain control. Strategic plans are projects and should be treated as such. In this book, we have given little credit to brilliant ideas that are not implemented. A plan that does not happen is merely that. Evaluation and feedback will ensure that our path to a better future occurs.

13

Where Do We Go from Here?

In order to add the material in this book to one's bag of tricks, it is necessary to practice it. As should be evident by now, we do not change our habits without practice. However, it is also possible to augment the material in this book with further reading. As mentioned in Chapter 1, reading is an excellent method of increasing creativity and the ability to respond to change. It makes us more aware of our problem-solving style and gives us insight on how to change it.

This chapter contains both bibliographic material on articles, books, and psychological experiments mentioned in the previous chapters and additional pertinent sources of information. The material is arranged in the order of the previous chapters in the book. The suggestions and comments are mine, and you may feel free to disagree with them at will. Thinking is an individual activity, and hopefully you do not think the way I do. Therefore I have undoubtedly omitted references that you feel are critical and included others that you consider to be criminally misleading. However, I can hardly write a book such as this and not take a little risk.

PREFACE

I mentioned best-selling books over the past few years that reflect concern with creativity and change. Four of these are: *Passages* by G. Sheehey (Bantam Books, N.Y., 1977), *Future Shock* by A. Toffler (Random House, N.Y., 1970), *The Fifth Generation* by E. Feigenbaum and P. McCorduck (Addison-Wesley, Reading, Mass., 1984), and *Megatrends* by J. Naisbitt (Warner Books, N.Y., 1984). There has also been an unusually large amount of material in newspapers and magazines about creativity and change. An example is the cover article "Are You Creative" in the September 30, 1985 issue of *Business Week*.

CHAPTER 1   AN INTRODUCTION TO CREATIVITY AND CHANGE

Two books mentioned in this chapter are: *How We Live* by V. Fuchs (Harvard University Press, Cambridge, Mass., 1983) and *The Social Psychology of Creativity* by T.M. Amabile (Springer-Verlag, N.Y., 1983). Although in this book I have been concerned with we normal people, if you are interested in reading about extremely creative people, find a copy of *The Creative Process* edited by B. Ghiselin (Mentor, N.Y., 1963), which is a collection of writings by extremely creative people (Mozart, Einstein, etc.) speaking about their own creative processes. Another one is *Essay on the Psychology of Invention in the Mathematical Field* by J. Hadamard (Dover, N.Y., 1954). This is a study of creativity among outstanding mathematicians and scientists. I find that books such as these are fascinating, but they unfortunately reinforce the inescapable conclusion that Mozart was more creative than I am.

CHAPTER 2   SOME THOUGHTS ABOUT THINKING

The comments about unconsciousness and creativity were from: M.M. Waldrop, "Before the Beginning" (*Science 84*, Jan/Feb 1984, American Association for the Advancement of Science), *Soul of a New Machine* by T. Kidder (Avon Books, N.Y., 1981), and S. Manna, "Pushing it to the Max" (*American Way*, June 25–July 8, 1985).

The books describing the philosophies of the various schools of psychology mentioned in the chapter are: *Philosophy of the Unconscious* by E. von Hartmann (2d edition, translated by W.C. Coupland, published by K. Paul, Tranch, Trubner and Co., London, 1893), *Principles of Psychology* by W. James (Dover, N.Y., 1950), *Interpretation of Dreams* by S. Freud (translated by A.A. Brill, Modern Library, N.Y., 1950), and *Psychology from the Standpoint of a Behaviorist* by J.B. Watson, (3d edition, J.B. Lippincott, Philadelphia, 1929).

The book that discusses sleep and dreaming is *Some Must Watch While Some Must Sleep* by W.C. Dement (Stanford Alumni Association, Stanford, Calif., 1977). An excellent discussion of historical attitudes toward unconscious thinking is *The Unconscious: Invention or Discovery?* by D.B. Klein (Goodyear Publishing Co., Santa Monica, Calif., 1977).

Five additional well-written books that discuss consciousness and unconsciousness are: *Altered States of Awareness* edited by T.J. Heyler (Readings from *Scientific American*, W.H. Freeman, N.Y., 1971), *The Psychology of Consciousness* by R.E. Ornstein (W.H. Freeman, N.Y., 1972), *The Mind's I* by D. Hofstadter and D. Dennett (Basic Books, N.Y., 1981), *The Psychology of Thought and Judgment* by D.M. Johnson (Harper and Brothers, N.Y., 1955), and *Gestalt Psychology* by W. Kohler (Liveright Publishing Corp., N.Y., 1947).

The first is a collection of articles that appeared in *Scientific American* during the fascination with altered states of consciousness during the late 1960s and early 1970s. The second deals with the right-brain, left-brain model. It conjectures upon its relation to Eastern philosophies and makes an argument for the integration of conventional psychology and physiology with what the author calls the traditional esoteric psychologies. The third is concerned with the Who am I? question.

As mentioned in Chapter 2, many psychologists have trouble with the concept of unconscious thinking because it is a most difficult topic for experiment. Two other related psychological concepts that seem to have found more acceptance are incubation and insight. The fourth book listed here reviews the psychological theories pertinent to problem solving until the mid-1950s and discusses the process of incubation and the evidence that supports it. The fifth book, representing the viewpoint of the gestalt psychologists, treats the topic of insight.

CHAPTER 3   THE MACHINERY OF THINKING

The information on limits of short-term memory is from B.A. Miller, "The Magical Number Seven Plus or Minus Two" (*Psychological Review* 63:81–97, 1956). A large amount of material on the mechanisms of the brain and nervous system is found in *A Second Level Course, Biology, Brains, and Behavior, Blocks A,B,C, and D* (Open University Press, Walton Hall, Milton Keynes, England, 1981).

Books and articles on the functional specialization of the brain are *Maps of the Mind* by C. Hampden Turner (Collier Books, N.Y., 1982), *Dragons of Eden* by C. Sagan (Random House, N.Y., 1977), *A Triune Concept of the Brain and Behavior* by P.D. Maclean (University of Toronto Press, Toronto, 1973), R.W. Sperry, "The Great Cerebral Commissure" (*Scientific American*, January 1964), and M.S. Gazzaniga, "The Split Brain in Man" (*Scientific American*, August 1967).

Two well-written books on the senses and sensors are: *Perception and the Senses* by E.L. Brown and K. Deffenbacher (Oxford University Press, N.Y., 1979) and *Sensation and Perception*, by H.R. Schiffman (2d edition, Wiley, N.Y., 1982). I relied upon them heavily for information on the senses that appears in the chapter.

The Einstein quote in the chapter was from the book by Jacques Hadamard referenced in Chapter 1.

A number of popular books on the brain have been written in the past few years. An excellent one, based on the also excellent PBS Television series "The Brain," is *The Brain* by R. Restak (Bantam Books, N.Y., 1984). Two others are: *The Brain Book* by P. Russell (Hawthorn Books, N.Y., 1979) and *The Universe Within* by M. Hunt (Simon & Schuster, N.Y., 1982).

Discussions of the brain and nervous system are also found in good introductory psychology books such as *Introduction to Psychology* by E. Hilgard, R. Atkinson, and R. Atkinson (7th edition, Harcourt Brace Jovanovich, N.Y., 1979) and *Psychology* by Henry Gleitman (W.W. Norton Co., N.Y., 1981).

CHAPTER 4   HABITS AND PROBLEM SOLVING

In a sense, the three previous chapters were background material for this one, and the majority of the readings are pertinent. If you want to read a historical book from a time when habit was blamed for most of our condition, take a look at *Habit* by W. James (H. Holt and Co., N.Y., 1914).

CHAPTER 5   MEMORY — BOXES OF INFORMATION

The experiment demonstrating visual recall from the sensory registers is described in G. Sperling, "The Information Available in Brief Visual Presentations" (*Psychological Monographs* 74, 1960). The experiment involving the picture of the traffic accident is from *Human Memory: The Processing of Information* by G.R. Loftus and E.F. Loftus (Halsted Press, N.Y., 1975).

The book about medical mnemonics is *Irving's Anatomy Mnemonics* by A.G. Smith (Churchill Livingstone, Edinburgh, 1983). The passage about the Viking is from *Memory* by I.M.L. Hunter (Penguin Books, Baltimore, 1974). Two good general books about memory and associated phenomena are: *Cognition* by A.R. Glass, K.J. Holyoak, and J.L. Santa (Addison-Wesley, Reading, Mass., 1979) and *Human Memory* by R.L. Klatsky (W.H. Freeman, N.Y., 1975).

CHAPTER 6   SPECIALIZATION AS A PROBLEM-SOLVING RESOURCE

An excellent although technical book on the way we perceive people is *Person Perception* by D.J. Schneider, A.H. Hastorf, and P.C. Ellsworth (2d edition, Addison-Wesley, Reading, Mass., 1979). The experiment having to do with perception of children is described in S.M. Dornbusch, A.H. Hastorf, S.A. Richardson, R.E. Muzzy, and R.S. Vreeland, "The Perceiver and Perceived: Their Relative Influence on Categories of Interpersonal Perception" (*Journal of Personality and Social Psychology*, 1:434–40, 1965). The decision-making game referred to in the chapter is "The Desert Survival Situation" by J. Clayton Lafferty in consultation with A.W. Pond. It is available from Human Synergistics, Plymouth, Michigan.

Readings having to do with the discussion of cognitive styles are: *Two Cultures and the Scientific Revolution* by C.P. Snow (Rede Lecture, Cambridge College, 1959), *Double Helix* by J. Watson (A Norton Critical Edition, edited by Gunther Stent, W.W. Norton, N.Y., 1980), *Man and His Symbols* by C.G. Jung, (Dell Publishing Co., N.Y., 1968), *Please Understand Me* by D. Keirsey and M. Bates (Prometheus Nemesis Book Company, Del Mar, Calif., 1984), and the Myers-Briggs Type Indicator, a test available to qualified professionals (training in testing) from the Consulting Psychologists Press, Palo Alto, Calif.

CHAPTER 7   OVERCOMING RUTS AND BOXES

The Polya checklist is from *How to Solve It* by G. Polya (Doubleday, N.Y., 1957). The Osborn checklist is from *Applied Imagination* by A. Osborn (Charles Scribner's Sons, N.Y., 1953). The pen design is from *The Universal Traveler* by D. Koberg and J. Bagnall (William Kaufmann Inc., Los Altos, Calif., 1974). The discussion of metaphor is from *Synectics* by W.J.J. Gordon (Harper & Row, N.Y., 1961).

There is a larger number of general creativity books that can be read in order to find more techniques and approaches to overcoming conceptual ruts. Some of these are: *Conceptual Blockbusting* by J.L. Adams (3d edition, Addison-Wesley, Reading, Mass., 1986), *Higher Creativity* by W. Harman and H. Rheingold (Jeremy Tarcher Inc., Los Angeles, 1984), *Wake Up Your Creative Genius* by K. Hanks and J.A. Parry (William Kaufmann Inc., Los Altos, Calif., 1983), *A Whack on the Side of the Head* by R. von Oech (Warner Books, N.Y., 1983), *Use Both Sides of Your Brain* by T. Buzan (E.P. Dutton, N.Y., 1976). *Training Your Creative Mind* by A.B. VanGundy (Prentice-Hall Inc., Englewood Cliffs, N.J., 1982), and *Imagineering* by M. LeBoeuf (McGraw-Hill Book Company, N.Y., 1980).

CHAPTER 8   TIME, MONEY, AND CREATIVITY

The statistics on R&D spending are from *Business Week*, July 8, 1985, pp. 86–106. You can easily conduct a personal experiment on this topic. Simply pick one of your personal projects that requires creativity and for the next few months devote twice as much time and money to it. You may find that you accomplish well over twice as much on it.

As far as the use of resources to promote creativity and change in groups and organizations, there has been a tremendous amount written on the management of research and development but not a great amount of study of the relationship between resources and creativity. It is a difficult topic because of the many variables involved and the impracticality of experimentation. Many organizations invest in research and development for reasons of faith; there seems to be agreement that it pays off. Also, their competitors do it. I obviously think that their faith is more than justified. The reader interested in economic factors having to do with corporate innovation should read *The Production and Application of New Industrial Technology* by E. Mansfield, J. Rapoport, A. Romeo, E. Villani, S. Wagner, and F. Husic (W.W. Norton & Company, N.Y., 1977), or *Technology Transfer, Productivity, and Economic Policy* by E. Mansfield, A. Romeo, M. Schwartz, D. Teece, S. Wagner, and P. Brach (W.W. Norton & Company, N.Y., 1982).

CHAPTER 9   EMOTION, RISK, AND PROBLEM SOLVING

The viewpoint of Kubie is from *Neurotic Distortions of the Creative Process* by L.S. Kubie (Farrar, Straus and Giroux, N.Y., 1966). Freud's view of creativity is found in *On Creativity and the Unconscious* by S. Freud (Harper & Row, N.Y., 1958). A discussion of behaviorism and behavior modification is found in most introductions to psychology textbooks, such as those mentioned in Chapter 3. These textbooks in turn list other sources. A classic book is *Principles of Behavior Modification* by A. Bandura (Holt, Rinehart & Winston, Inc., N.Y., 1969). The Carnegie-Mellon data is from "Education in the Arts and Sciences: Divergent Paths," the Ph.D. dissertation of Robert Altemeier done at Carnegie-Mellon in 1965.

CHAPTER 10   REWARDS — THE NECESSARY POT OF GOLD

The experiment that asked people to match line lengths is described in S.E. Asch, "Studies of Independence and Conformity; A Minority of One Against a Unanimous Majority" (*Psychological Monographs* 70 (9, Whole No. 416), 1956).

Like Chapters 4 and 8, this chapter is based upon a large amount of the reading in the previous chapters. In particular, the psychological readings are pertinent. The Amabile book mentioned in Chapter 1 is excellent on the topic of intrinsic reward, and behavior modification has much to say about extrinsic rewards. Once again, introductory psychology textbooks reference many specialized works on needs, psychological stages, and other human characteristics of importance in properly utilizing reward systems to promote creativity and responsiveness to change.

CHAPTER 11   PULLING TOGETHER — ORGANIZING FOR
CREATIVITY

The curve used in conjunction with Mr. Greiner's thoughts is from L. Greiner, "Evolution and Revolution as Organizations Grow," *Harvard Business Review*, July–August 1972, pp. 37–45. An interesting book to read about some of the difficulties of creativity in large organizations is *The Mythical Man Month* by F.P. Brooks, Jr., (Addison-Wesley, Reading, Mass., 1982). The classical work on Theory X-Theory Y is *The Human Side of Enterprise* by Douglas MacGregor (McGraw-Hill Book Company, N.Y., 1960). The experiment having to do with willingness to become involved is from J. Darley and B. Latane, "Bystander Intervention in Emergencies: Diffusion of Responsibility" (*Journal of Personality and Social Psychology* 10:202–14, 1968).

The experiment having to do with the rewarded job is from J. Festinger and J. M. Carlsmith, "Cognitive Consequences of Forced Compliance (*Journal of Abnormal and Social Psychology* 58:203–10, 1959).

The do's and don'ts figure is from G.M. Prince, *Synectics: Twenty-Five Years of Research into Creativity and Group Process* (a publication of the American Society for Training and Development). A classic general book on organizational behavior is *Managerial Psychology* by H. Leavitt (4th edition, University of Chicago Press, Chicago, 1978).

CHAPTER 12   DECISION MAKING AND STRATEGY

There are many books on analytical decision making, often called the decision sciences in the business sector. A good introductory textbook is *Quantitative Analysis for Business Decisions* by H. Bierman, C.P. Bonini, and W.H. Hausman (6th edition, Richard Irwin, Homewood, Ill., 1981). The Kepner-Tregoe book is *The New Rational Manager* by C.H. Kepner and B.B. Tregoe (Kepner-Tregoe, Inc., Princeton, N.J., 1981).

The following books are about strategy. They are written for people in companies but contain messages for small groups and individuals: *Strategies for Change: Logical Incrementalism*, by J.B. Quinn (Irwin Inc., Homewood, Ill., 1980), *Competitive Strategy* by M.E. Porter (The Free Press, N.Y., 1980), *Strategic Planning in Emerging Companies* by S.C. Brandt (Addison-Wesley, Reading, Mass., 1981), *Organizational Transitions* by R. Beckhard and R. Harris, (Addison-Wesley Publishing Co., Reading, Mass., 1977), *The Art of Japanese Management* by R.T. Pascale and A.G. Athos (Simon & Schuster, N.Y., 1981), and *Competitive Strategic Management*, edited by R.B. Lamb (Prentice-Hall, Englewood Cliffs, N.J., 1984).

Index